THE EARLY HUMAN WORLD

WORLD

TEACHING GUIDE

OXFORD

UNIVERSITY PRESS

OXFORD
UNIVERSITY PRESS

Oxford University Press, Inc., publishes works that
further Oxford University's objective of excellence
in research, scholarship, and education.

Oxford   New York
Auckland   Cape Town   Dar es Salaam   Hong Kong   Karachi
Kuala Lumpur   Madrid   Melbourne   Mexico City   Nairobi
New Delhi   Shanghai   Taipei   Toronto

With offices in
Argentina   Austria   Brazil   Chile   Czech Republic   France   Greece
Guatemala   Hungary   Italy   Japan   Poland   Portugal   Singapore
South Korea   Switzerland   Thailand   Turkey   Ukraine   Vietnam

Copyright © 2005 by Oxford University Press, Inc.

Published by Oxford University Press, Inc.
198 Madison Avenue, New York, NY, 10016
www.oup.com

Writer: Susan Moger
Editor: Robert Weisser
Project Editor: Lelia Mander
Project Director: Jacqueline A. Ball
Education Consultant: Diane L. Brooks, Ed.D.
Design: Design Lab NYC

Casper Grathwohl, Publisher

ISBN-13: 978-0-19-522281-4 (California edition)   ISBN-13: 978-0-19-517897-5

Printed in the United States
on acid-free paper

CONTENTS

NOTE TO THE TEACHER

Dear Educator:

You probably love history. You read historical novels, watch documentaries, and enjoy (and, as a history teacher, no doubt criticize) Hollywood's attempts to recreate the past. So why don't most kids love history too? We think it might be because of the tone of the history books they are assigned. Many textbook authors seem to assume that the sole goal of teaching history is to make sure the students memorize innumerable facts. So, innumerable facts are crammed onto the pages, facts without context, as thrilling to read as names in a phone book.

Real history, however, is not just facts; it's the story of real people who cared deeply about the events and controversies of their times. And learning real history is essential. It helps children to understand the events that brought the world to where they find it now. It helps them distrust stereotypes of other cultures. It helps them read critically. (It also helps them succeed in standardized assessments of their reading skills.) We, like you, find history positively addictive. Students can feel the same way. (Can you imagine a child reading a history book with a flashlight after lights out, just because it is so interesting?)

The World in Ancient Times books reveal ancient history to be a great story—a whole bunch of great stories—some of which have been known for centuries, but some of which are just being discovered. Each book in the series is written by a team of two writers: a scholar who is working in the field of ancient history and knows what is new and exciting, and a well-known children's book author who knows how to communicate these ideas to kids. The teams have come up with books that are historically accurate and up to date as well as beautifully written. They also feature magnificent illustrations of real artifacts, archaeological sites, and works of art, along with maps and timelines to allow readers to get a sense of where events are set in place and time. Etymologies from the *Oxford English Dictionary*, noted in the margins, help to expand students' vocabulary by identifying the ancient roots, along with the meanings, of English words.

The authors of our books use vivid language to describe what we know and to present the evidence for *how* we know what we know. We let the readers puzzle right along with the historians and archaeologists. The evidence comes in the form of primary sources, not only in the illustrations but especially in the documents written in ancient times, which are quoted extensively.

You can integrate these primary sources into lessons with your students. When they read a document or look at an artifact or building in the illustrations they can pose questions and make hypotheses about the culture it came from. Why was a king shown as much larger than his attendants in an Egyptian relief sculpture? Why was Pliny unsure about what to do with accused Christians in his letter to the emperor? In this way, students can think like historians.

The series provides a complete narrative for a yearlong course on ancient history. You might choose to have your students read all eight narrative books as they learn about each of the civilizations in turn (or fewer than eight, depending on the ancient civilizations covered in your school's curriculum). Or you might choose to highlight certain chapters in each of the books, and use the others for extended activities or research projects. Since each chapter is written to stand on its own, the students will not be confused if you don't assign all of them. The *Primary Sources and Reference Volume* provides longer primary sources than are available in the other books, allowing students to make their own interpretations and comparisons across cultures.

The ancient world was the stage on which many institutions that we think of as modern were first played out: law, cities, legitimate government, technology, and so on. The major world religions all had their origins long ago, before 600 CE, as did many of the great cities of the world. *The World in Ancient Times* presents this ancient past in a new way—new not just to young adults, but to any audience. The scholarship is top-notch and the telling will catch you up in the thrill of exploration and discovery.

Amanda H. Podany and Ronald Mellor
General Editors, *The World in Ancient Times*

THE WORLD IN ANCIENT TIMES PROGRAM

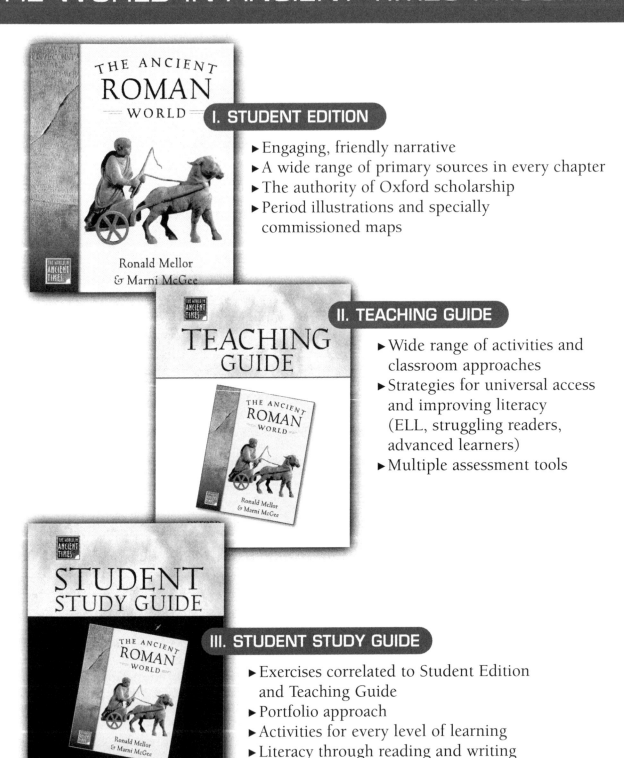

I. STUDENT EDITION

- Engaging, friendly narrative
- A wide range of primary sources in every chapter
- The authority of Oxford scholarship
- Period illustrations and specially commissioned maps

II. TEACHING GUIDE

- Wide range of activities and classroom approaches
- Strategies for universal access and improving literacy (ELL, struggling readers, advanced learners)
- Multiple assessment tools

III. STUDENT STUDY GUIDE

- Exercises correlated to Student Edition and Teaching Guide
- Portfolio approach
- Activities for every level of learning
- Literacy through reading and writing

PRIMARY SOURCES AND REFERENCE VOLUME

- Broad selection of primary sources in each subject area
- Ideal resource for in-class exercises and unit projects

TEACHING GUIDE: KEY FEATURES

The Teaching Guides organize each *The World in Ancient Times* book into units, usually of three or four chapters each. The chapters in each unit cover a key span of time or have a common theme, such as a civilization's origins, government, religion, economy, and daily life.

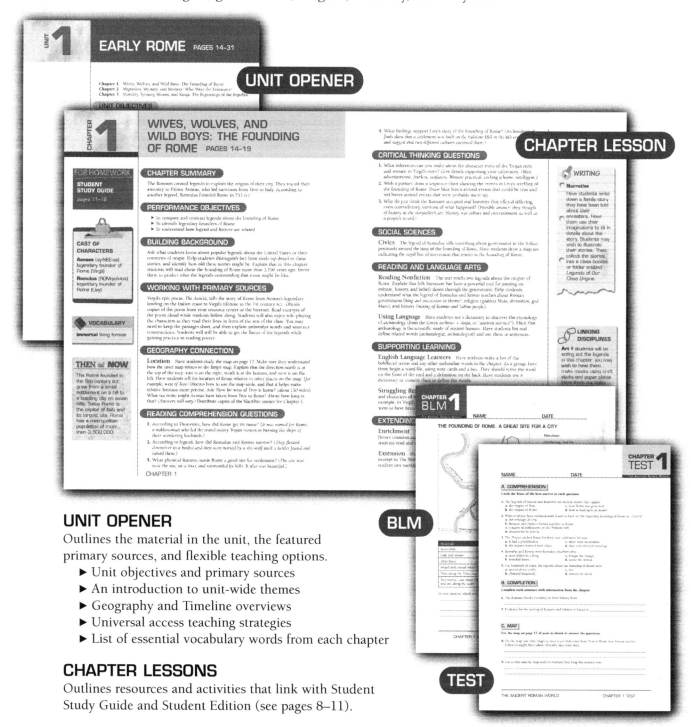

UNIT OPENER

Outlines the material in the unit, the featured primary sources, and flexible teaching options.

▶ Unit objectives and primary sources
▶ An introduction to unit-wide themes
▶ Geography and Timeline overviews
▶ Universal access teaching strategies
▶ List of essential vocabulary words from each chapter

CHAPTER LESSONS

Outlines resources and activities that link with Student Study Guide and Student Edition (see pages 8–11).

TESTS AND BLACKLINE MASTERS (BLMS)

Reproducible tests and exercises for assessment, homework, or classroom projects

Organized so that you can easily find the information you need.

CHAPTER SUMMARY AND PERFORMANCE OBJECTIVES

The Chapter Summary gives an overview of the information in the chapter. The Performance Objectives are the three or four important goals students should achieve in the chapter. Accomplishing these goals will help students master the information in the book.

BUILDING BACKGROUND

This section connects students to the chapter they are about to read. Students may be asked to use what they know to make predictions about the text, preview the images in the chapter, or connect modern life with the ancient subject matter.

WORKING WITH PRIMARY SOURCES

A major feature of *The World in Ancient Times* is having students read about history through the words and images of the people who lived it. Each book includes excerpts from the best sources from these ancient civilizations, giving the narrative an immediacy that is difficult to match in secondary sources. Students can read further in these sources on their own or in small groups using the accompanying *The World in Ancient Times Primary Sources and Reference Volume*. The Teaching Guide recommends activities so students of all skill levels can appreciate the ways people from the past saw themselves, their ideas and values, and their fears and dreams.

CHAPTER 1

WIVES, WOLVES, AND WILD BOYS: THE FOUNDING OF ROME   PAGES 14–19

FOR HOMEWORK

STUDENT STUDY GUIDE
pages 11–12

CAST OF CHARACTERS

Aeneas (ay-NEE-us)
legendary founder of Rome (Virgil)

Romulus (ROM-yuh-lus)
legendary founder of Rome (Livy)

VOCABULARY

immortal living forever

THEN and **NOW**

The Rome founded in the 8th century BCE grew from a small settlement on a hill to a bustling city on seven hills. Today Rome is the capital of Italy and its largest city. Rome has a metropolitan population of more than 3,500,000.

CHAPTER SUMMARY

The Romans created legends to explain the origins of their city. They traced their ancestry to Prince Aeneas, who led survivors from Troy to Italy. According to another legend, Romulus founded Rome in 753 BCE.

PERFORMANCE OBJECTIVES

- ► To compare and contrast legends about the founding of Rome
- ► To identify legendary founders of Rome
- ► To understand how legend and history are related

BUILDING BACKGROUND

Ask what students know about popular legends about the United States or their countries of origin. Help students distinguish fact from made-up detail in these stories, and identify how old these stories might be. Explain that in this chapter students will read about the founding of Rome more than 2,700 years ago. Invite them to predict what the legends surrounding that event might be like.

WORKING WITH PRIMARY SOURCES

Virgil's epic poem, *The Aeneid*, tells the story of Rome from Aeneas's legendary landing on the Italian coast to Virgil's lifetime in the 1st century BCE. Obtain copies of the poem from your resource center or the Internet. Read excerpts of the poem aloud while students follow along. Students will also enjoy role-playing the characters as they read their lines in front of the rest of the class. You may need to keep the passages short, and then explain unfamiliar words and sentence constructions. Students will still be able to get the flavor of the legends while gaining practice in reading poetry.

GEOGRAPHY CONNECTION

Location   Have students study the map on page 17. Make sure they understand how the inset map relates to the larger map. Explain that the direction north is at the top of the map, east is on the right, south is at the bottom, and west is on the left. Have students tell the location of Rome relative to other places on the map. (*for example, west of Troy*) Discuss how to use the map scale, and that it helps make relative location more precise. Ask: How far west of Troy is Rome? (*about 750 miles*) What sea route might Aeneas have taken from Troy to Rome? About how long is that? (*Answers will vary.*) Distribute copies of the blackline master for Chapter 1.

READING COMPREHENSION QUESTIONS

1. According to Dionysius, how did Rome get its name? (*It was named for Roma, a noblewoman who led the travel-weary Trojan women in burning the ships of their wandering husbands.*)
2. According to legend, how did Romulus and Remus survive? (*They floated downriver in a basket and then were nursed by a she-wolf until a herder found and raised them.*)
3. What physical features made Rome a good site for settlement? (*The site was near the sea, on a river, and surrounded by hills. It also was beautiful.*)

CHAPTER 1

GEOGRAPHY CONNECTION

Each chapter has a Geography Connection to strengthen students' map skills as well as their understanding of how geography affects human civilization. One of the five themes of geography (Location, Interaction, Movement, Place, and Regions) is highlighted in each chapter. Map skills such as reading physical, political, and historical maps; using latitude and longitude to find locations; and using the features of a map (mileage scale, legend) are taught throughout the book and reinforced in blackline masters.

4. What findings support Livy's story of the founding of Rome? (*Archaeological finds show that a settlement was built on the Palatine Hill in the 8th century BCE and suggest that two different cultures coexisted there.*)

CRITICAL THINKING QUESTIONS

1. What inferences can you make about the character traits of the Trojan men and women in Virgil's story? Give details supporting your inferences. (*Men: adventuresome, fearless, seafarers. Women: practical, seeking a home, intelligent.*)
2. With a partner, draw a sequence chart showing the events in Livy's retelling of the founding of Rome. Draw blue boxes around events that could be true and red boxes around events that were probably made up.
3. Why do you think the Romans accepted oral histories that offered differing, even contradictory, versions of what happened? (*Possible answer: they thought of history as the storyteller's art. History was culture and entertainment as well as a people's record.*)

SOCIAL SCIENCES

Civics   The legend of Romulus tells something about government in the Italian peninsula around the time of the founding of Rome. Have students draw a diagram indicating the royal line of succession that results in the founding of Rome.

READING AND LANGUAGE ARTS

Reading Nonfiction   The text retells two legends about the origins of Rome. Explain that folk literature has been a powerful tool for passing on culture, history, and beliefs down through the generations. Help students understand what the legend of Romulus and Remus teaches about Roman government (king and succession to throne), religion (goddess Vesta, divination, god Mars), and history (mixing of Roman and Sabine people).

Using Language   Have students use a dictionary to discover the etymology of *archaeology* (from the Greek *archaio-* + *-logia*, or "ancient science"). Elicit that archaeology is the scientific study of ancient humans. Have students list and define related words (*archaeologist, archaeological*) and use them in sentences.

SUPPORTING LEARNING

English Language Learners   Have students make a list of the boldfaced terms and any other unfamiliar words in the chapter. As a group, have them begin a word file, using note cards and a box. They should write the word on the front of the card and a definition on the back. Have students use a dictionary or context clues to define the words.

Struggling Readers   Have students make a chart comparing the events and characters of the two legends. Then help students draw conclusions: for example, in Virgil, the founders of Rome came from Troy; in Livy, the founders seem to have been living in Italy already.

EXTENDING LEARNING

Enrichment   Edith Hamilton's book *Mythology: Timeless Tales of Gods and Heroes* contains another myth about the founding of Rome by Aeneas. Have students read and summarize this myth for the class.

Extension   Have student groups act out scenes from *The Aeneid*, from the excerpt in *The World in Ancient Times Primary Sources and Reference Volume*. One student can narrate while the others take the parts of the characters involved.

THE ANCIENT ROMAN WORLD

WRITING

Narrative

Have students write down a family story they have been told about their ancestors. Have them use their imaginations to fill in details about the story. Students may wish to illustrate their stories. Then collect the stories into a class booklet or folder entitled *Legends of Our Class Origins.*

LINKING DISCIPLINES

Art If students will be acting out the legends in this chapter, you may wish to have them make masks using craft sticks and paper plates. Have them cut holes for eyes and mouth. They can model their characters' features after the pictures of Roman men and women in Chapters 1–3.

READING COMPREHENSION AND CRITICAL THINKING QUESTIONS

The reading comprehension questions are general enough to allow free-flowing class or small group discussion, yet specific enough to be used for oral or written assessment of students' grasp of the important information. The critical thinking questions are intended to engage students in a deeper analysis of the text and can also be used for oral or written assessment.

SOCIAL SCIENCES ACTIVITIES

Students can use these activities to connect the subject matter in the Student Edition with other areas in the social sciences: economics, civics, and science, technology, and society.

READING AND LANGUAGE ARTS

These activities serve a twofold purpose: Some are designed to facilitate the development of nonfiction reading strategies. Others can be used to help students' appreciation of fiction and poetry, as well as nonfiction, by dealing with concepts such as word choice, description, and figurative language.

SUPPORTING LEARNING AND EXTENDING LEARNING

Each chapter gives suggestions for students of varying abilities and learning styles; for example, advanced learners, below-level readers, auditory/visual/tactile learners, and English language learners. These may be individual, partner, or group activities, and may or may not require your ongoing supervision.
(For more on Supporting or Extending Learning sections, see pages 16–19.)

Icons quickly help to identify key concepts, facts, activities, and assessment activities in the sidebars.

▶ Cast of Characters/Vocabulary

These sidebars point out and identify bolded, curriculum-specific vocabulary words and significant personalities in the chapter. Pronunciation guides are included where necessary. Additional important vocabulary words are listed in each unit opener.

▶ Writing

Each chapter has a suggestion for a specific writing assignment. You can make these assignments as you see fit—to help students meet state requirements in writing as well as to help individual students improve their skills. Areas of writing covered include the following:

Description	Personal writing (journal/diary)
Narration	News article (print and electronic)
Explanation	Dialogue
Persuasion	Interview
Composition	Poetry

▶ Then and Now

This feature provides interesting facts and ideas about the ancient civilization and relates it to the modern world. This may be an aspect of government that we still use today, word origins of common modern expressions, physical reminders of the past that are still evident, and other features. You can use this item simply to promote interest in the subject matter or as a springboard to other research.

▶ Linking Disciplines

This feature offers opportunities to investigate other subject areas that relate to the material in the Student Edition: math, science, arts, and health. Specific areas of these subjects are emphasized: **Math** (arithmetic, algebra, geometry, data, statistics); **Science** (life science, earth science, physical science); **Arts** (music, arts, dance, drama, architecture); **Health** (personal health, world health).

▶ For Homework

A quick glance links you to additional activities in the Student Study Guide that can be assigned as homework.

ASSESSMENT

The World in Ancient Times program intentionally omits from the Student Edition the kinds of section, chapter, and unit questions that are used to review and assess learning in standard textbooks. It is the purpose of the series to engage readers in learning—and loving—history written as good literature. Rather than interrupting student reading, and enjoyment, all assessment instruments for the series have been placed in the Teaching Guides.

▶ CHAPTER TESTS

A reproducible chapter test follows each chapter in this Teaching Guide. These tests will help you assess students' mastery of the content standards addressed in each chapter. These tests measure a variety of cognitive and analytical skills, particularly comprehension, critical thinking, and expository writing, through multiple choice, short answer, and essay questions.

An answer key for the chapter tests is provided at the end of the Teaching Guide.

▶ WRAP-UP TEST

After the last chapter test you will find a wrap-up test consisting of 10 essay questions that evaluate students' ability to synthesize and express what they've learned about the ancient civilization under study.

▶ RUBRICS

The rubrics at the back of this Teaching Guide will help you assess students' written work, oral presentations, and group projects. They include a Scoring Rubric, based on the California State Public School standards for good writing and effective cooperative learning. In addition, a simplified hand-out is provided, plus a form for evaluating group projects and a Library/Media Center Research Log to help students focus and evaluate their research. Students can also evaluate their own work using these rubrics.

▶ BLACKLINE MASTERS (BLMs)

A blackline master follows each chapter in the Teaching Guide. These BLMs are reproducible pages for you to use as in-class activities or homework exercises. They can also be used for assessment as needed.

▶ ADDITIONAL ASSESSMENT ACTIVITIES

Each unit opener includes suggestions for using one or more unit projects for assessment. These points, and the rubrics provided, will help you evaluate how your students are progressing towards meeting the unit objectives.

USING THE STUDENT STUDY GUIDE FOR ASSESSMENT

▶ Study Guide Activities

Assignments in the Student Study Guide correspond with those in the Teaching Guide. If needed, these Student Study Guide activities can be used for assessment.

▶ Portfolio Approach

Student Study Guide pages can be removed from the workbook and turned in for grading. When the pages are returned, they can be part of the students' individual history journals. Have students keep a 3-ring binder portfolio of Study Guide pages, alongside writing projects and other activities.

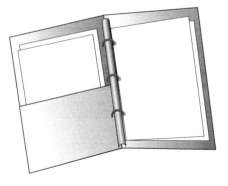

The Student Study Guide works as both standalone instructional material and as a support to the Student Edition and this Teaching Guide. Certain activities encourage informal small-group or family participation. These features make it an effective teaching tool:

Flexibility

You can use the Study Guide in the classroom, with individuals or small groups, or send it home for homework. You can distribute the entire guide to students; however, the pages are perforated so you can remove and distribute only the pertinent lessons.

A page on reports and special projects in the front of the Study Guide directs students to the Further Reading resource in the student edition. This feature gives students general guidance on doing research and devising independent study projects of their own.

FACSIMILE SPREAD

The Study Guide begins with a facsimile spread from the Student Edition. This spread gives reading strategies and highlights key features: captions, primary sources, sidebars, headings, etymologies. The spread supplies the contextualization students need to fully understand the material.

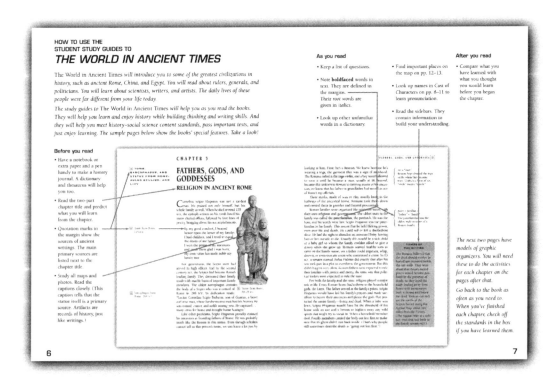

Portfolio Approach

The Study Guide pages are three-hole-punched so they can be integrated with notebook paper in a looseleaf binder. This history journal or portfolio can become both a record of content mastery and an outlet for each student's unique creative expression. Responding to prompts, students can write poetry or songs, plays and character sketches, create storyboards or cartoons, or construct multi-layered timelines.

The portfolio approach gives students unlimited opportunities for practice in areas that need strengthening. Students cam share their journals and compare their work. And the Study Guide pages in the portfolio make a valuable assessment tool for you. It is an ongoing record of performance that can be reviewed and graded periodically.

GRAPHIC ORGANIZERS

This feature contains reduced models of seven graphic organizers referenced frequently in the guide. Using these devices will help students organize the material so it is meaningful to them. (Full-size reproducibles of each graphic organizer are provided at the back of this Teaching Guide.) These graphic organizers include: outline, main idea map, K-W-L chart (What I Know, What I Want to Know, What I Learned), Venn diagram, timeline, sequence of events chart, and T-chart.

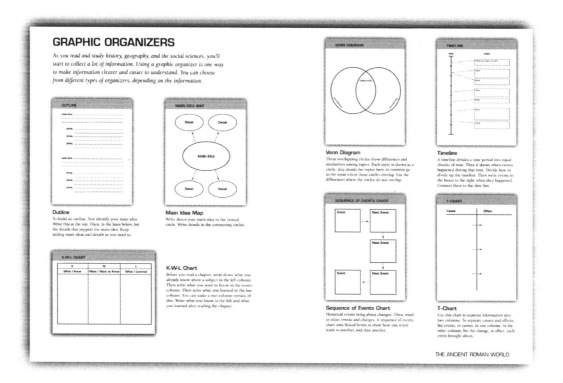

STUDENT STUDY GUIDE: **CHAPTER LESSONS**

Each chapter lesson is designed to draw students into the subject matter. Recurring features and exercises challenge their knowledge and allow them to practice valuable analysis skills. Activities in the Teaching Guide and Student Study Guide complement but do not duplicate each other. Together they offer a wide range of class work, group projects, and opportunities for further study and assessment that can be tailored to all ability levels.

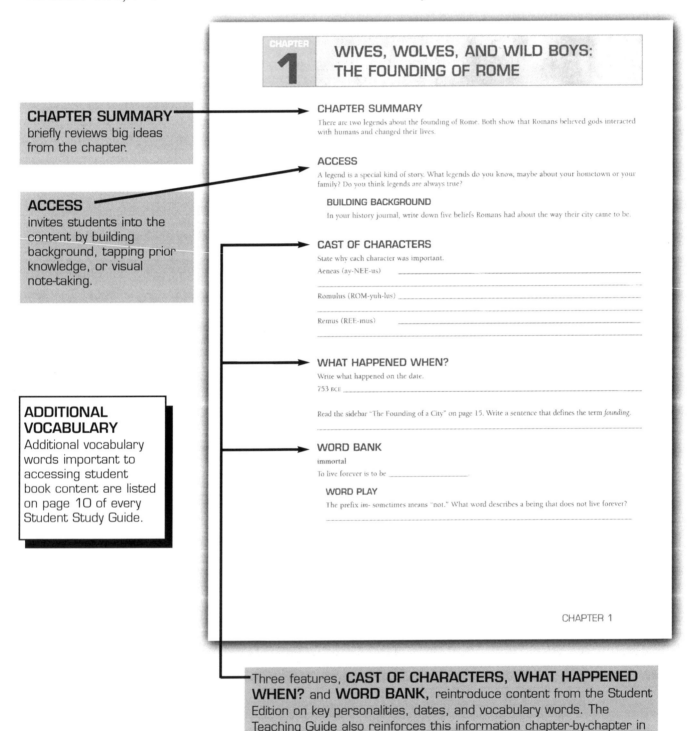

CHAPTER SUMMARY
briefly reviews big ideas from the chapter.

ACCESS
invites students into the content by building background, tapping prior knowledge, or visual note-taking.

ADDITIONAL VOCABULARY
Additional vocabulary words important to accessing student book content are listed on page 10 of every Student Study Guide.

CHAPTER 1

WIVES, WOLVES, AND WILD BOYS: THE FOUNDING OF ROME

CHAPTER SUMMARY
There are two legends about the founding of Rome. Both show that Romans believed gods interacted with humans and changed their lives.

ACCESS
A legend is a special kind of story. What legends do you know, maybe about your hometown or your family? Do you think legends are always true?

BUILDING BACKGROUND
In your history journal, write down five beliefs Romans had about the way their city came to be.

CAST OF CHARACTERS
State why each character was important.
Aeneas (ay-NEE-us) _____

Romulus (ROM-yuh-lus) _____

Remus (REE-mus) _____

WHAT HAPPENED WHEN?
Write what happened on the date.
753 BCE _____

Read the sidebar "The Founding of a City" on page 15. Write a sentence that defines the term *founding*.

WORD BANK
immortal
To live forever is to be _____.

WORD PLAY
The prefix *im-* sometimes means "not." What word describes a being that does not live forever?

_____

CHAPTER 1

Three features, **CAST OF CHARACTERS, WHAT HAPPENED WHEN?** and **WORD BANK,** reintroduce content from the Student Edition on key personalities, dates, and vocabulary words. The Teaching Guide also reinforces this information chapter-by-chapter in the VOCABULARY and CAST OF CHARACTERS sidebars.

CRITICAL THINKING
CAUSE AND EFFECT

Draw a line from each cause and connect it to the result, or effect. (There is one extra effect.)

CAUSE	EFFECT
1. Amulius feared he would be overthrown,	a. they floated down the river and were saved by a she-wolf.
2. Rhea Silvia broke her vows,	b. the Romans and Sabines went to war.
3. A servant couldn't kill the babies,	c. Romulus killed Remus.
4. Remus made fun of Romulus,	d. Romans and Sabines called a truce
5. Romulus's men kidnapped Sabine women,	e. Romulus and Remus were born.
6. The Sabine women ran onto the battlefield,	f. he forced Rhea Silvia to join the Vestal Virgins.
	g. Remus killed Romulus.

WITH A PARENT OR PARTNER

When you have completed the chart, read aloud each cause-and-effect pairing to a parent or partner. Use the word "so" to connect each cause with each effect.

WRITE ABOUT IT

The Trojan women were *appalled* that Aeneas and the Trojan men were planning another journey after they reached the mouth of the Tiber River. To be *appalled* means to be

a) happy
b) excited
c) shocked

Circle your answer.

In your history journal, write a short dialogue or a descriptive scene between the Trojan men and women about making this second journey. Why were the women appalled? How did the men respond?

WORKING WITH PRIMARY SOURCES

The image at left is an ancient Roman coin. It shows an image of a Roman god. Think about what we can learn about ancient cultures through artifacts like this one. Answer the following questions in your history journal.

1. Why do you think the figure is wearing an olive wreath?
2. Why would the Romans put a god on their coins?
3. What famous people do we use on coins today? (It's okay to take a peek at your pocket change!)
4. If people found your coins hundreds of years from now, what conclusions might they draw about your culture?
5. Think up a design for your own coin and draw it in your history journal.

THE ANCIENT ROMAN WORLD

CRITICAL THINKING exercises draw on such thinking skills as establishing cause and effect, making inferences, drawing conclusions, determining sequence of events, comparing and contrasting, identifying main ideas and details, and other analytical process.

WRITE ABOUT IT gives students writing suggestions drawn from the material. A writing assignment may stem from a vocabulary word, a historical event, or a reading of a primary source. The assignment can take any number of forms: newspaper article, letter, short essay, a scene with dialogue, a diary entry.

WORKING WITH PRIMARY SOURCES invites students to read primary sources closely. Exercises include answering comprehension questions, evaluating point of view, and writing and other forms of creative expression, including music, art, and design. "In Your Own Words" writing activities ask students to paraphrase a primary source.

The books in this series are written in a lively, narrative style to inspire a love of reading history–social science. English language learners and struggling readers are given special consideration within the program's exercises and activities. And students who love to read and learn will also benefit from the program's rich and varied material. Following are strategies to make sure each and every student gets the most out of the subjects you will teach through *The World in Ancient Times*.

ENGLISH LANGUAGE LEARNERS

For English learners to achieve academic success, the instructional considerations for teachers include two mandates:

- Help them attain grade level, content area knowledge, and academic language.
- Provide for the development of English language proficiency.

To accomplish these goals, you should plan lessons that reflect the student's level of English proficiency. Students progress through five developmental levels as they increase in language proficiency:

Beginning and Early Intermediate (*grade level material will be mostly incomprehensible, students need a great deal of teacher support*)

Intermediate (*grade level work will be a challenge*)

Early Advanced and Advanced (*close to grade level reading and writing, students continue to need support*)

The books in this program are written at the intermediate level. However, you can still use the lesson plans for students of different levels by using the strategies below:

Tap Prior Knowledge
What students know about the topic will help determine your next steps for instruction. Using K-W-L charts, brainstorming, and making lists are ways to find out what they know. English learners bring a rich cultural diversity into the classroom. By sharing what they know, students can connect their knowledge and experiences to the course.

Set the Context
Use different tools to make new information understandable. These can be images, artifacts, maps, timelines, illustrations, charts, videos, or graphic organizers. Techniques such as role-playing and story-boarding can also be helpful. Speak in shorter sentences, with careful enunciation, expanded explanations, repetitions, and paraphrasing. Use fewer idiomatic expressions.

Show—Don't Just Tell
English learners often get lost as they listen to directions, explanations, lectures, and discussions. By showing students what is expected, you can help them participate more fully in classroom activities. Students need to be shown how to use the graphic organizers in this guide and the mini versions in the student study guide, as well as other blackline masters for note-taking and practice. An overhead transparency with whole or small groups is also effective.

Use the Text

Because of unfamiliar words, students will need help. Teach them to preview the chapter using text features (headings, bold print, sidebars, italics). See the suggestions in the facsimile of the Student Edition, shown on pages 6–7 of the Student Study Guide. Show students organizing structures such as cause and effect or comparing and contrasting. Have students read to each other in pairs. Encourage them to share their history journals with each other. Use Read Aloud/Think Aloud, perhaps with an overhead transparency. Help them create word banks, charts, and graphic organizers. Discuss the main idea after reading.

Check for Understanding

Rather than simply ask students if they understand, stop frequently and ask them to paraphrase or expand on what you just said. Such techniques will give you a much clearer assessment of their understanding.

Provide for Interaction

As students interact with the information and speak their thoughts, their content knowledge and academic language skills improve. Increase interaction in the classroom through cooperative learning, small group work, and partner share. By working and talking with others, students can practice asking and answering questions.

Use Appropriate Assessment

When modifying the instruction, you will also need to modify the assessment. Multiple choice, true and false, and other criterion reference tests are suitable, but consider changing test format and structure. English learners are constantly improving their language proficiency in their oral and written responses, but they are often grammatically incorrect. Remember to be thoughtful and fair about giving students credit for their content knowledge and use of academic language, even if their English isn't perfect.

STRUGGLING READERS

Some students struggle to understand the information presented in a textbook. The following strategies for content-area reading can help students improve their ability to make comparisons, sequence events, determine importance, summarize, evaluate, synthesize, analyze, and solve problems.

Build Knowledge of Genre

Both the fiction and narrative nonfiction genres are incorporated into *The World in Ancient Times*. This combination of genres makes the text interesting and engaging. But teachers must be sure students can identify and use the organizational structures of both genres.

Fiction	Nonfiction
Each chapter is a story	Content: historical information
Setting: historical time and place	Organizational structure: cause/effect, sequence of events, problem/solution
Characters: historical figures	Other features: maps, timelines, sidebars, photographs, primary sources
Plot: problems, roadblocks, and resolutions	

In addition, the textbook has a wealth of the text features of nonfiction: bold and italic print, sidebars, headings and subheadings, labels, captions, and "signal words" such as *first*, *next*, and *finally*. Teaching these organizational structures and text features is essential for struggling readers.

Build Background

Having background information about a topic makes reading about it so much easier. When students lack background information, teachers can preteach or "front load" concepts and vocabulary, using a variety of instructional techniques. Conduct a chapter or book walk, looking at titles, headings, and other text features to develop a big picture of the content. Focus on new vocabulary words during the "walk" and create a word bank with illustrations for future reference. Read aloud key passages and discuss the meaning. Focus on the timeline and maps to help students develop a sense of time and place. Show a video, go to a website, and have trade books and magazines on the topic available for student exploration.

Comprehension Strategies

While reading, successful readers are predicting, making connections, monitoring, visualizing, questioning, inferring, and summarizing. Struggling readers have a harder time with these "in the head" processes. The following strategies will help these students construct meaning from the text until they are able to do it on their own.

> **PREDICT:** Before reading, conduct a picture and text feature "tour" of the chapter to make predictions. Ask students if they remember if this has ever happened before, to predict what might happen this time.

> **MAKE CONNECTIONS:** Help students relate content to their background (text to text, text to self, and text to the world).

> **MONITOR AND CONFIRM:** Encourage students to stop reading when they come across an unknown word, phrase, or concept. In their notebooks, have them make a note of text they don't understand and ask for clarification or figure it out. While this activity slows down reading at first, it is effective in improving skills over time.

> **VISUALIZE:** Students benefit from imagining the events described in a story. Sketching scenes, story-boarding, role-playing, and looking for sensory details all help students with this strategy.

> **INFER:** Help students look beyond the literal meaning of a text to understand deeper meanings. Graphic organizers and discussions provide opportunities to broaden their understanding. Looking closely at the "why" of historical events helps students infer.

> **QUESTION AND DISCUSS:** Have students jot down their questions as they read, and then share them during discussions. Or have students come up with the type of questions they think a teacher would ask. Over time students will develop more complex inferential questions, which lead to group discussions. Questioning and discussing also helps students see ideas from multiple perspectives and draw conclusions, both critical skills for understanding history.

DETERMINE IMPORTANCE: Teach students how to decide what is most important from all the facts and details in nonfiction. After reading for an overall understanding, they can go back to highlight important ideas, words, and phrases. Clues for determining importance include bold or italic print, signal words, and other text features. A graphic organizer such as a main idea map also helps.

Teach and Practice Decoding Strategies

Rather than simply defining an unfamiliar word, teach struggling readers decoding strategies:

- Have them look at the prefix, suffix, and root to help figure out the new word.

- Look for words they know within the word.

- Use the context for clues, and read further or reread.

ADVANCED LEARNERS

Every classroom has students who finish the required assignments and then want additional challenges. Fortunately, the very nature of history and social science offers a wide range of opportunities for students to explore topics in greater depth. Encourage them to come up with their own ideas for an additional assignment. Determine the final product, its presentation, and a timeline for completion.

▶ Research

Students can develop in-depth understanding through seeking information, exploring ideas, asking and answering questions, making judgments, considering points of view, and evaluating actions and events. They will need access to a wide range of resource materials: the Internet, maps, encyclopedias, trade books, magazines, dictionaries, artifacts, newspapers, museum catalogues, brochures, and the library. See the Further Reading section at the end of the Student Edition for good jumping-off points.

▶ Projects

You can encourage students to capitalize on their strengths as learners (visual, verbal, kinesthetic, or musical) or to try a new way of responding. Students can prepare a debate or write a persuasive paper, play, skit, poem, song, dance, game, puzzle, or biography. They can create an alphabet book on the topic, film a video, do a book talk, or illustrate a book. They can render charts, graphs, or other visual representations. Allow for creativity and support students' thinking.

Cheryl A. Caldera, M.A.
Literacy Coach

UNIT OBJECTIVES

Unit 1 spans billions of years, from the beginning of planet Earth and the first signs of life through the appearance of the first hominids and their place in Darwin's hypothesis about the relationship between humans and apes. In this unit, your students will learn

▶ how Earth and its moon developed as part of the solar system.
▶ how fossils are formed.
▶ what fossils have so far told us about the earliest hominids.
▶ to recognize the relative position of humans and chimpanzees on the *Hominoidea* family "bush."

PRIMARY SOURCES

Unit 1 includes pictures of artifacts or excerpts from the following primary sources:

▶ Earth's moon
▶ snail fossil
▶ horseshoe crab fossil
▶ root-ape ancestor jaw bone
▶ root-ape ancestor big toe bone
▶ root-ape ancestor tooth
▶ Charles Darwin, *The Descent of Man,* 1871
▶ Charles Darwin, *Expressions of Emotions of Man and Animals,* 1873

BIG IDEAS IN UNIT 1

Change, evolution, and **diversity** are the big ideas presented in Unit 1. The unit discusses the changes that occurred over billions of years and resulted in the first life on Earth. It details the diversity of life on Earth millions of years ago and describes how evolution is a way of describing the connection between hominids, modern chimpanzees, and humans.

To introduce these ideas, ask students what they think they know about Earth's origins and place in the solar system. Then elicit their understanding of the evolution of life on Earth. Allow students to express their diverse opinions.

GEOGRAPHY CONNECTION

Refer students to the maps on page 17 and discuss the changes that they show. You may want to provide more detailed information about Pangaea and plate tectonics.

TIMELINE

14 billion years ago	Solar system forms
4.5 billion years ago	Moon breaks off from Earth
3.6 billion years ago	Earliest life on Earth
3 billion years ago	First land forms on Earth
5.5 million years ago	Earliest hominids live in what is now Ethiopia

UNIT PROJECTS

Earth in Motion

Invite a team of students to create giant puzzle pieces shaped liked the continents of 135 million years ago. Have them use the maps on page 17 for this project. In a presentation set to majestic classical music, the team can first stand with the puzzle pieces touching (as in the map labeled "135 million years ago"), then slowly move apart (65 million years ago), and finally separate into the present-day configuration. One or two students can serve as narrators. To expand this project to include the whole class, have different groups report on how the continental plates moved around during different periods in the earth's history. Instruct student groups to build models or maps using color-coded moveable pieces to represent how the continents have shifted over time.

Tectonic Plates Today

Ask a group of students to report on tectonic plate action today. One area of interest to scientists is the Mid-Atlantic Ridge. Students can find information from print resources or from the US Geological Survey's website at *http://pubs. usgs.gov/publications/text/understanding.html.*

Chimpanzees and Language

Invite interested students to find out more about chimpanzees' use of sign language. Expert readers will find information on the Internet at *www.mnsu. edu/emuseum/cultural/language/chimpanzee.html.* Students can create a presentation for the class using this and other sources.

Darwin—In His Own Words

A small group of students can access excerpts from Darwin's *Voyage of the Beagle,* an account of his groundbreaking explorations in the Galapagos Islands starting in 1831. The excerpts can be found at *www.pbs.org/wgbh/evolution/educators/ teachstuds/pdf/darwins_excerpts.pdf.* Students can choose four or five paragraphs that reveal Darwin's interests and how he conducted observations. They can then read the excerpts aloud to the class, explaining why they chose them.

ADDITIONAL ASSESSMENT

For Unit 1, divide the class into groups and have them all undertake the Tectonic Plates Today project so that you can assess their understanding of how the earth continues to change. Use the scoring rubric at the back of this guide to assess students' work, and have students rate their own work with the self-assessment rubric.

LITERATURE CONNECTION

There are numerous enjoyable books that will broaden students' knowledge of Darwin's theory and of humans and chimpanzees.

- ▶ Goodall, Jane. *In the Shadow of Man*. Boston: Mariner Books, 2000. Nonfiction. Jane Goodall gives an account of her first assignment to study chimpanzees in the Gombe Stream Reserve. ADVANCED
- ▶ Morgan, Jennifer, and Dana Lynne Andersen. *Born with a Bang: The Universe Tells Our Cosmic Story*. Nevada City, Ca.: Dawn Publications, 2002. Nonfiction. This story opens with the very beginning of the universe and ends with the formation of Earth. AVERAGE
- ▶ ——. *From Lava to Life: The Universe Tells Our Earth's Story*. Nevada City, Ca.: Dawn Publications, 2003. Nonfiction. A sequel to *Born with a Bang,* this book picks up the story with the first appearance of life on Earth. AVERAGE
- ▶ Sis, Peter. *The Tree of Life: Charles Darwin*. Boston: Farrar, Straus & Giroux, 2003. Nonfiction. This richly illustrated book takes a look at the life, studies, and ideas of Charles Darwin. EASY

UNIVERSAL ACCESS

The following strategies are designed to cover a range of learning styles and reading, language, and skill levels. You may find that students of all abilities will benefit from the various strategies presented.

Reading Strategies

- ▶ To facilitate reading, point out features such as illustrations, information, and definitions in the side columns that students will encounter as they read. For example, in Chapter 1, point out the definition of *hominid* on page 19, and in Chapter 2, page 21, the sidebar How to Become a Fossil.

- ▶ There will be many unfamiliar words in these chapters. Before reading a chapter, point out potentially difficult words and ask volunteers to pronounce and define them. Say each word several times and then write it on the board. Help students associate the spoken word with the written word.

- ▶ Call on students to read sections of the chapters aloud. For example, in Chapter 1 they can read aloud the "calendar year" timeline starting with the first paragraph on page 19; or, in Chapter 3, the excerpts from primary sources on page 29. Encourage students to use expressive intonation and hand gestures where appropriate. Fit the reading passage to the abilities of each student.

Writing Strategies

- ▶ Have partners make a three-column chart with headings for each of the unit's big ideas. Partners should get together after reading each chapter to jot down their observations in each category.

- ▶ Have students make a compare-and-contrast chart titled *How Are Humans and Apes Similar and Different?* They should list two or three similarities and differences and explain why they chose to include particular information.

- ▶ Have students create a cause-and-effect chart based on the "How to Become a Fossil" sidebar on page 21.

Listening and Speaking Strategies

▶ As you read portions of the chapters, call on volunteers to describe what they think the scenes looked like. For example, students could describe or act out Haile-Selassie's discovery of a hominid jaw bone (page 22–23). They could convey the thrill Haile-Selassie says he felt and the reaction the other workers had to his discovery.

▶ Have students look at the illustration at the bottom of page 18 and describe what it depicts. Then have them explain how the artist knew what today's deserts looked like 34 million years ago.

UNIT VOCABULARY LIST

The following words that appear in Unit 1 are important for your students' understanding of the social studies content as well as for development of literacy. Use these words for vocabulary study or to reinforce language arts skills (e.g., synonyms, compound words, prefixes and suffixes, and related words). Words are listed below in the order in which they appear in each chapter.

Chapter 1	Chapter 2	Chapter 3
smithereens	scrubland	swagger
gravity	scavengers	ferocious
careen	radioactive	aggression
pockmarked	trowel	deduction
rotation	evolution	instinct
volcanic	climate	naturalist
torrents	periodically	mimic
crater	hostile	natural selection
comet	environmental	anthropoid
asteroid		extinct
tectonic		species
plumes		unwieldy
turbulence		organism

**STUDENT
STUDY GUIDE**

pages 11–12

VOCABULARY

hominid a member of the family of mammals called *Hominidae*. Humans are the only surviving hominids.

THEN and NOW

The "Ring of Fire" is the name for a line of active volcanoes around the Pacific Rim. The ring includes over 50 percent of the world's active volcanoes above sea level and is marked by frequent earthquakes and volcanic eruptions. Locate some of these volcanoes on a world map for the class.

CHAPTER SUMMARY

Earth emerged from the swirling chaos of the Big Bang 14 billion years ago and underwent many cataclysmic changes before our remotest ancestors emerged.

PERFORMANCE OBJECTIVES

▶ To understand some of the events that resulted in the creation of the Earth and moon
▶ To recognize the first signs of life on Earth
▶ To appreciate that humans have been on Earth a relatively short time

BUILDING BACKGROUND

Ask students what they know about time travel and time machines from books, movies, video games, or other sources. Tell them that this chapter starts all the way back 14 billion years ago and is written as a trip forward in time. Have students give their impressions of what the universe might have been like at that time.

WORKING WITH PRIMARY SOURCES

On the board, copy the dates from the timeline on page 15. Have students complete the timeline by adding dates for the fossils shown on pages 17 and 18. Ask students if they have seen a snail or a horseshoe crab. Explain that today those animals look like fossils of their ancestors that are millions of years old.

GEOGRAPHY CONNECTION

Location   Have students find the shapes of South America and Africa in the first map on page 17. Ask them to look at the next two maps and trace the changes that led up to the relative positions of the two continents today.

READING COMPREHENSION QUESTIONS

1. What role did comets and asteroids play in the development of life on Earth? (*Space dust from comets and asteroids provided atoms and chemicals necessary for life.*)
2. Describe what Earth's surface looked like 225 million years ago. (*There was a single land mass—the supercontinent, Pangaea—surrounded by water.*)
3. What feature is constant (unchanged) in all four maps on page 17? (*the Equator*)
4. Distribute copies of the blackline master for Chapter 1. Have students complete the activity, placing the events described in Chapter 1 in the correct order.

CRITICAL THINKING QUESTIONS

1. Which came first: snails or horseshoe crabs? How do we know? (*snails; from dating fossils that have been found*)

2. What were some of the results of continents' crashing into each other? (*Mountains were thrust up, the earth's crust crinkled, and volcanoes erupted.*)

3. Using the "all-time calendar" on page 19, compare the time it took for Earth to form with the length of time hominids have been on Earth. (*It took until September for the Earth to form. By contrast, hominids appeared on Earth only in the last four hours of the last day of the year.*)

SOCIAL SCIENCES

Science, Technology, and Society   Students can investigate and report on the Hubble telescope's investigation of the Big Bang—the event believed to have started the universe and ultimately formed our sun and Earth. They can find information on the NASA website at *www.nasa.gov/vision/ universe/starsgalaxies/hubble_UDF.html.*

READING AND LANGUAGE ARTS

Reading Nonfiction   Have students note the timeline on page 15 and the historical map on page 17. Elicit what information these features add to the text. Explain that students will see many more of these kinds of features in this book.

Using Language   Work with students to recognize the verbs ending in *-ing* in the first and second paragraphs on page 15 (*circling, flying, crashing, nudging, thinning, crumpling, sucking, smoothing, joining*). Students should then explain how these verbs help them visualize the chaos of the early solar system.

SUPPORTING LEARNING

Struggling Readers   To emphasize how short a time human history is relative to the age of the Earth, underline students' understanding of "10 seconds." Give a start signal and ask students to raise their hands when they estimate 10 seconds have passed. Then do a countdown of 10 seconds so students have a sense of how long it is. Ask students to calculate what percentage 10 seconds is of the school day and of the calendar year.

EXTENDING LEARNING

Enrichment   Have a small groups investigate how scientists are using data from radar from a satellite to gain new insights into tectonic movements. They can find information from the European Space Agency online at *www. eurekalert.org/pub_releases/2004-08/esa-erv080604.php.*

Extension   Have students use a simple jigsaw puzzle (several large pieces) to demonstrate how tectonic plates move on the Earth's surface.

WRITING

Persuasion Have students write an ad promoting travel in the "all-time" vehicle that gave them their view of the formation of Earth. In their ads, students should promote the comfort of the ride and the exciting experiences of the trip, such as interplanetary collisions, fireballs, freezing temperatures, and boiling heat.

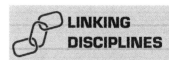

LINKING DISCIPLINES

Music Play selections from a recording of Gustav Holst's *The Planets* as a "sound track" to the chapter, especially pages 14–16.

NAME   DATE

SEQUENCING EARTH'S MILESTONES

Directions

As you read Chapter 1, use this organizer to identify how long ago each of these events occurred. The earliest and most recent events in this list have been filled in.

Event	Approximate Number of Years Ago
Big Bang	14 billion
Sun begins to shine	
Moon splits off from Earth	
Space dust jump-starts life on Earth	
First land forms on Earth	
All land on Earth is located in southern part of globe	
Snails exist on Earth	
Pangaea begins to break up	
Horseshoe crab appears	
Dinosaurs exist on Earth	
Asteroid hits Earth; dinosaurs die out	
Monkey-like primates exist in Egyptian rainforest	
Hominids appear	6 million

NAME   **DATE**

A. MULTIPLE CHOICE

Circle the letter of the best answer for each question.

1. Which of the following is **not** part of the early history of the world?
   a. The moon splits off from Earth.
   b. All land on Earth forms one big continent.
   c. Dinosaurs and hominids roam Earth together.
   d. Continents collide and mountains are built.

2. Land started forming on Earth about
   a. 14 billion years ago.   **c.** 3 billion years ago.
   b. 65 million years ago.   **d.** 3 million years ago.

3. The end of the dinosaur age was the result of
   a. an asteroid hitting Earth.   **c.** a huge explosion on the sun.
   b. water covering most of Earth. **d.** an asteroid hitting the moon.

4. Over 3.5 billion years ago, space dust with life-building chemicals came to Earth
   a. riding on comets and asteroids. **c.** from the sun.
   b. from the moon.   **d.** along with lava from deep inside Earth.

5. Thirty-four million years ago, the land that is now Egypt was a
   a. hot, sandy desert.   **c.** lush rainforest.
   b. volcanic island.   **d.** frozen wasteland.

B. SHORT ANSWER

Write one or two sentences to answer each question.

6. How were the planets of our solar system formed?

_____

_____

7. How is the Earth's thin crust different from the shell of an egg?

_____

_____

8. How did the supercontinent of 225 million years ago become the seven continents of today?

_____

_____

C. ESSAY

On a separate sheet of paper, write an essay explaining this statement from the chapter: "Almost everything we know about humans from written history happens in that last ten-second countdown—10, 9, 8, 7 . . ." Use details from the chapter to support your main idea.

THE BIG DIG: THE EARLIEST HOMINIDS—SO FAR PAGES 20–24

CAST OF CHARACTERS

Ardipithecus ramidus kadabba (ar-dee-PITH-eh-kus RAM-eh-dus kad-ABBA) earliest known hominid, lived in Ethiopia 5.8–4.3 million years ago

Yohannes Haile-Selassie (YO-hahn HI-lee-sell-ASS-ee) Ethiopian anthropologist who found earliest known hominid

Giday WoldeGabriel (gi-DAY WAHL-duh gab-ree-EL) Ethiopian geologist who works with Yohannes Haile-Selassie

hominid member of a family of mammals that walked on two legs

Toumai (too-MY) name given to fossil skull found in Chad that may belong to an early hominid

Orrorin tugenensis (oar-ROAR-in TOO-gen-en-sis) candidate for earliest hominid; fragments of fossils have been found in Kenya

CHAPTER SUMMARY

Chapter 2 introduces an important point about the study of the distant past—that paleontological and paleoanthropological discoveries are the result of weeks, months, and even years of painstaking work. The chapter gives two scientists' descriptions of the oldest hominid fossils.

PERFORMANCE OBJECTIVES

▶ To understand the process of fossil formation
▶ To identify and describe the evidence of life that fossils provide
▶ To understand the significance of the discovery of root-ape ancestor fossils

BUILDING BACKGROUND

Talk with students about their experience with painstaking work such as gardening, model-building, or doing research in a library or online. What did they find difficult about concentrating on a task for a long time? What did they enjoy about the process? Explain that in this chapter they will meet two scientists whose patience paid off with a spectacular discovery.

WORKING WITH PRIMARY SOURCES

Have students look at the fossil pictures on page 23 and ask them to explain why each of the photographs shows a person's fingers holding a fossil. (*The hand gives a sense of the relative size of each fossil.*)

GEOGRAPHY CONNECTION

Location Ask students to use the map on page 20 to help them locate the Middle Awash Valley in Ethiopia on a larger map of Africa. Have students identify the absolute and relative location of the valley. (*The Awash River can be found at about 8° N 44° E. It is in Ethiopia and flows from the mountains near Addis Ababa northeastward through Africa's Rift Valley, ending at Lake Abhe on the Djibouti border.*)

READING COMPREHENSION QUESTIONS

1. What were scholars Yohannes Haile-Selassie and Giday WoldeGabriel and their students doing in the Middle Awash Valley? (*looking for fossils of hominids*)
2. What kinds of fossils did they find? (*monkey skull, antelope horn, hominid teeth, jaw bone, and toe bones*)
3. What was Haile-Selassie able to learn about the root-ape ancestor from the fossils he found? (*Root-ape walked the same way we do and ate leaves and fruit.*)
4. Distribute copies of the blackline master for Chapter 2. Have students complete the activity, matching fossils with descriptions of their significance.

CRITICAL THINKING QUESTIONS

1. How do volcanoes help fossil hunters? (*Volcanic ash and lava cover, trap, and preserve animals and plants for fossil hunters to find. Since volcanic rock can be dated, fossil hunters can date the fossils they find in volcanic rock.*)

2. How does erosion in the Awash Valley help scientists like Haile-Selassie find fossils? (*Erosion from wind and rain exposes fossils that have been buried for millions of years.*)

3. What was the Awash Valley area like when root-ancestor lived there? How is it different today? (*Then it was a moist, lush forest. Today it is a hot desert.*)

4. Why do you think scientists are so eager to discover the "earliest" hominid? (*possible answers: the desire to find evidence of our hominid ancestors; the ambition to be the one who finds evidence to fill in the gaps in our knowledge of the past*)

SOCIAL SCIENCES

Economics   The chapter describes a dig undertaken by a geologist, an anthropologist, and their students camped in the Awash Valley. Have students describe the costs of an expedition like this. They don't need to give exact costs in dollars but rather list categories of expenses and with the general reasons for each.

READING AND LANGUAGE ARTS

Reading Nonfiction   The sidebars in this chapter show how complicated an archaeologists job is. Have students draw conclusions about why there are so many questions about the earliest hominids even after decades of research.

Using Language   Have students read over the list of *-ologies* on page 20 and add other words with that suffix to the list (for example, *sociology, psychology, biology*). Then have them research and write their own chart of word origins and meanings.

SUPPORTING LEARNING

English Language Learners   Draw students' attention to the Cast of Characters on pages 9–11. Show them how to use the pronunciations. Familiarize them with the sounds by having them sound out and write their own names using the pronunciation guide.

Struggling Readers   Have students make a timeline of Haile-Selassie's actions on the day he found the root-ancestor's jawbone.

EXTENDING LEARNING

Enrichment   Students can learn more about the discovery of *Ardipithecus ramidus kadabba* by visiting *www.berkeley.edu/news/berkeleyan/2001/07/11_homin. html*. Have students report their findings to the class.

Extension   Simulate a fossil discovery by bringing in a paper sack of foam packing peanuts. Cover up the picture side of several puzzle pieces and place them in the sack of peanuts along with paper clips, erasers, and other non-fossils. Explain that students will "dig" by touch for the fossils (puzzle pieces). After students find the puzzle pieces, they fit them together. Only then can they claim a fossil discovery.

WRITING

Dialogue Have students write and present a dialogue between two scientists discussing whether Toumai (page 24) is the earliest hominid or an ape.

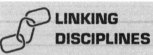

LINKING DISCIPLINES

Arts Have pairs of students work together to draw a picture of the site of Haile-Selassie's dig that is described on page 22. Or have all students contribute to a class mural.

THEN and NOW

In March 2004, Yohannes Haile-Selassie and other researchers reported in the journal *Science* their discovery of six new fossil teeth in the area where *Ardipithecus ramidus kadabba* was found. The six tooth fossils have resulted in the renaming of the original hominid as a species in its own right—*Ardipithecus ramidus kadabba.*

NAME _____ **DATE** _____

LEARNING FROM FOSSILS

Directions

WoldeGabriel and Haile-Selassie found numerous fossils in the Middle Awash Valley of Ethiopia. For each fossil listed below, explain the conclusions these scientists could draw about *Ardipithecus ramidus kadabba* or the environment in which the root-ape lived. Use complete sentences.

Fossils Discovered at Middle Awash Valley	Conclusions
piece of monkey skull	
antelope horn	
toe bone	
teeth	

A. MULTIPLE CHOICE

Circle the letter of the best answer for each question.

1. Which of the following was **not** found in the dig in the Middle Awash Valley?
   a. part of a jawbone
   b. piece of a monkey skull
   c. complete hominid skull
   d. several toe bones

2. Six million years ago the area where *Ardipithecus ramidus kadabba* was found looked like
   a. the ocean floor.
   b. a lush forest.
   c. a sheet of ice.
   d. a desert.

3. Volcanoes are good for fossil making for all these reasons **except**
   a. the noise of an eruption scares away living things.
   b. radioactive material in volcanic rock can be dated.
   c. volcanic ash covers and preserves what it falls on.
   d. flowing lava traps anything in its path.

4. Which statement best describes how Haile-Selassie discovered the tooth and jawbone of *Ardipithecus ramidus kadabba*?
   a. He found it on the ground.
   b. He recognized a pattern in a layer of rock.
   c. He dug it from a pit.
   d. He stepped on it by accident.

5. *Ardipithecus ramidus kadabba* lived among what animals?
   a. elephants, horses, and monkeys
   b. buffalo, cats, dogs
   c. dinosaurs
   d. horseshoe crabs and snails

B. SHORT ANSWER

Write one or two sentences to answer each question.

6. How is a fossil of an ancient bone formed?

   _____

   _____

7. At an archaeological dig, how can you tell the age of fossils that you find?

   _____

   _____

8. How did Haile-Selassie's find contradict other scientists' views about the first hominids?

   _____

   _____

C. ESSAY

Write an essay on a separate sheet of paper summarizing the significance to the picture of human evolution of discovering *Ardipithecus ramidus kadabba*.

FOR HOMEWORK

STUDENT STUDY GUIDE

pages 15–16

CAST OF CHARACTERS

Chimpanzees at Burgers' Zoo a captive colony of common chimpanzees being observed by scholars

Jane Goodall (GOOD-awl) scientist who has devoted most of her life to the study and conservation of chimpanzees

 VOCABULARY

quadruped an animal that walks on four feet

taxonomy grouping living things according to their relationships with one another

CHAPTER SUMMARY

Close observations of our nearest relatives, chimpanzees, support Charles Darwin's theories about the similarities between apes and humans, who share a common ancestor.

PERFORMANCE OBJECTIVES

▶ To understand how the social behavior of chimpanzees is similar to that of humans
▶ To understand Darwin's theory of natural selection
▶ To compare characteristics of chimpanzees and humans

BUILDING BACKGROUND

Ask students if they have ever heard that chimpanzees have been taught to "talk" using sign language. Explain that this chapter will introduce a group of chimpanzees whose achievements overshadow even that milestone.

WORKING WITH PRIMARY SOURCES

Read aloud the excerpt from *The Expressions of Emotions of Man and Animals* quoted on page 29. Discuss whether students agree with Darwin's followers who thought he had gone too far in light of the chimpanzee "emotions" described in the chapter.

GEOGRAPHY CONNECTION

Region   Have students research where chimpanzees, humankind's "closest living relatives," live, and whether their number are increasing or declining. A good source of information is *www.tc.umn.edu/~joha0103/chimp.html*.

READING COMPREHENSION QUESTIONS

1. Why are scientists studying the behavior of chimpanzees at Burgers' Zoo? What are they discovering? (*They are trying to understand the social life of chimps and are discovering how much like humans they are.*)
2. What did Darwin believe about the connection between apes and humans? (*that they share a common ancestor*)
3. What does the science of taxonomy do? (*organizes living things in relation to each other*)
4. Distribute copies of the blackline master for Chapter 3. Have students complete the Venn diagram comparing the characteristics of chimpanzees and humans.

CRITICAL THINKING QUESTIONS

1. What was the significance of the chimpanzees' escape from Burgers' Zoo? (*The escape showed that the chimps could reason, imitate the actions of others, and use tools.*)

2. What did Darwin mean when he said "Man is descended from a hairy . . . quadruped"? (*He meant that modern humans and apes shared a common ancestor before they split into two separate lines of descent, not that modern humans are descended from modern apes.*)

3. What is the significance of chimpanzees' behavior when they look in a mirror? (*Unlike other animals, chimpanzees seem to know they are seeing themselves, not another animal, when they look in a mirror. That makes them more like humans than any other animal.*)

4. Why do the authors say, "Darwin would not have been surprised" at the escape of the Burgers' Zoo chimps? (*Darwin said apes could reason, make tools, imitate, and remember—all of which are qualities that are needed for an effective escape.*)

SOCIAL SCIENCES

Science, Technology, and Society   Have students consider the specific examples of chimpanzee behavior described in this chapter in light of Darwin's belief that apes could "reason and use tools." Then have them explain how the examples do or do not support Darwin's belief.

READING AND LANGUAGE ARTS

Reading Nonfiction   This chapter mostly treats the similarities between humans and chimpanzees. Have students outline the information in the chapter, using the categories of similarities (emotions, use of tools, reason, and so on) as the main topics, and including details for each one.

SUPPORTING LEARNING

English Language Learners   Have a small group read one of the following chimpanzee scenes from the chapter aloud and then retell it from memory. The scenes might be "The Rock Band" (page 25), "Jimmie's Game" (page 27), "The Escape" (third paragraph, page 27), or "Gorilla's New Baby" (second paragraph, page 31).

Struggling Readers   Use the information in the first paragraph on page 30 along with the taxonomy chart on page 31 to reinforce that humans are not descended from chimpanzees but rather share a common ancestor from the superfamily *Hominoidea*.

EXTENDING LEARNING

Enrichment   Students can use the Internet to learn more about taxonomy, specifically other groupings in which humans appear, by visiting *www.msu.edu/ ~nixonjos/armadillo/taxonomy.html* and *www.umanitoba.ca/anthropology/courses/ 121/primatology/taxonomy.html*. Have students make up a taxonomic table from their findings.

Extension   Read the section on page 29 describing Washoe's mastery of sign language. Have students go to *www.masterstech-home.com/ASLDict.html* to learn some words in American Sign Language. Discuss how hard it was for them to learn to sign and what they think of the fact that Washoe learned to sign 300 words.

WRITING

Narrative Have students observe a human activity (e.g., students in the cafeteria, on a school bus, in the gym, at a sporting event, or dancing) and then write a letter describing the activity as if they were seeing it for the first time. They can refer to the description of a football game on page 26.

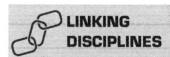

LINKING DISCIPLINES

Arts Have students redraw the taxonomy chart as a tree showing how chimpanzees and humans branched off from the common tree trunk *Hominoidea* as two branches, *Pongidae* and *Hominidae*, which in turn branch into *Pan* and *Homo* and again into *troglodytes* (common chimp) and *sapiens*.

NAME   **DATE**

COMPARING CHIMPANZEES AND HUMANS

Directions

From the list of characteristics, choose those that describe only humans, only chimpanzees, or both. Write the letter of each characteristic in the appropriate section of the Venn diagram. Use the information in Chapter 3 as a reference.

A. use sign language	**H.** recognize selves in a mirror
B. use keys	**I.** faces are not flat
C. walk on four feet	**J.** play games
D. communicate by speaking	**K.** bigger brain than other group
E. kiss friends good-bye	**L.** make simple tools
F. read	**M.** walk on two feet
G. enjoy eating termites	**N.** more hairy than other group

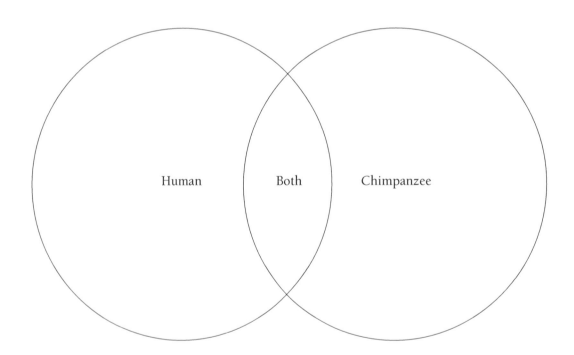

NAME   **DATE**

A. MULTIPLE CHOICE

Circle the letter of the best answer for each question.

1. Which of the following is **not** a behavior of chimpanzees at Burgers' Zoo?
    a. planning escape   **c.** reading magazines
    b. picking keepers' pockets   **d.** playing drums

2. Which statement best describes Charles Darwin's hypothesis about the relationship between humans and apes?
    a. Apes like to be tickled.   **c.** Animals express emotions.
    b. They have nothing in common.   **d.** They have a common ancestor.

3. Which statement sums up the reactions of scientists to Darwin in his lifetime?
    a. No scientist ever thought he went too far.
    b. Scientists everywhere cheered the theory of natural selection.
    c. Many scientists believed in Darwin's idea of evolution.
    d. No scientists ever questioned his theory.

4. Which statement best describes how chimpanzees respond to their reflection in a mirror?
    a. They hide from it.   **c.** They try to break the mirror.
    b. They act like it is another animal.   **d.** They use the mirror to look at themselves.

5. Which statement best defines *taxonomy*?
    a. the science of grouping living things to show relationships
    b. the art of stuffing and mounting dead animals
    c. the science of studying chimpanzees in the wild
    d. the art of teaching sign language to chimpanzees

B. SHORT ANSWER

Write one or two sentences to answer each question.

6. How did Charles Darwin explain humans' relationship to apes?

_____

_____

7. What does chimpanzees' use of tools show about their ability to reason?

_____

_____

8. Explain Darwin's theory of natural selection.

_____

_____

C. ESSAY

Chapter 3 says, "The evolutionary process . . . behaves more like a bush, branching off in all directions. . . . Many of the twigs come to dead ends, representing extinct species. Some continue to divide as new species branch off from their parents." Write an essay explaining how the bush and branching twig model explains the similarities and differences between humans and chimpanzees.

HOMINIDS: THE OLDEST OF THE OLD—SO FAR

UNIT OBJECTIVES

Unit 2 covers discoveries of hominid evidence in Africa from 3.5-million-year-old bipeds' footsteps to 1.6-million-year-old Turkana Boy. In this unit, your students will learn

▶ how scientists discovered the earliest bipedal hominids, and the significance of bipedalism.
▶ the significance of the discoveries of Lucy (*Australopithecus afarensis*) and Garhi (*Australopithecus garhi*).
▶ the significance of evidence that hominids butchered animals in Olduvai Gorge 1.8 million years ago.
▶ about the discovery of Turkana Boy (*Homo erectus*).

PRIMARY SOURCES

Unit 2 includes pictures of the following artifacts:

▶ Fossilized footprint, Tanzania, 3.6 million years ago
▶ Fossilized horse jaw, Ethiopia, 3.2 million years ago
▶ *Australopithecus afarensis* skeleton, Ethiopia, 3.2 million years ago
▶ *Australopithecus afarensis* bones, Ethiopia, 3.5–3 million years ago
▶ *Australopithecus garhi* skull, Ethiopia, 2.5 million years ago
▶ Flake tool, Ethiopia, 2.3 million years ago
▶ *Australopithecus boisei* skull, Tanzania, 1.8 million years ago
▶ Fossils and artifacts, Olduvai, Tanzania, 1.75 million years ago
▶ *Homo erectus* skull of Turkana Boy, Kenya, 1.6 million years ago
▶ *Homo erectus* vertebrae of Turkana Boy, Kenya, 1.6 million years ago

BIG IDEAS IN UNIT 2

Discovery, change, evolution, and **diversity** are the big ideas presented in Unit 2. In Africa, scientists have made thrilling discoveries that advance our knowledge of humans' earliest ancestors, the hominids. The fossil evidence documents changes such as hominids' walking on two legs and evolving in bone size and diet from a vegetarian-only diet to one that includes meat. The fossil evidence reveals diverse bipedal hominids, some of whom had sophisticated toolmaking skills.

You may want to introduce these ideas by eliciting students' ideas about scientific discovery. Ask: What do we mean by a scientific "breakthrough"? What changes in thinking does a breakthrough or discovery require? Are people always receptive to new discoveries? Why do scientific discoveries lead to further questions?

GEOGRAPHY CONNECTION

Refer students to the map on pages 12 and 13 and provide more detailed maps of Africa. Have students draw a map of Africa showing the locations of early archaeological finds.

TIMELINE

3.6 million years ago	Early hominids leave footprints at Laetoli, Tanzania
3.18 million years ago	Lucy (*Australopithecus afarensis*) lives and dies in Ethiopia
2.5 million years ago	First use of stone tools by *Australopithecus garhi* in East Africa
1.8 million years ago	Earliest occupation of Olduvai Gorge, Tanzania
1.6 million years ago	Turkana Boy (*Homo erectus*) lives and dies in Kenya

UNIT PROJECTS

Making Footprints

Scientists discovered the footprints of three hominids who walked through volcanic mud 3.6 million years ago in Africa. Ask students to make their own "footprints" to leave for future archaeologists. They can cut an extra-large footprint shape from a large sheet of paper. On it, they can record their height and foot size. Use this information to compile a chart to be used in a class discussion about the relationship between height and footprint size. Also have them list evidence about themselves that future archaeologists could discover. This could be a list of five to ten favorite possessions. Have students sign and date their footprints and keep them in a safe place. Then ask students to write a response to the following question: If your footprint were discovered years from now, what conclusions would an archaeologist draw about your life?

Bipedal Benefits

Have a group of students create an infomercial touting the benefits of walking upright. Some students will act as the bipedal presenters, who will create props to make their point. Other students will play the audience of skeptical hominids who prefer moving as quadrupeds. Audience members can raise objections typical of those who favor the status quo. Have the group present its finalized infomercial to the class.

Make a Mobile

Invite students to demonstrate the relative ages of various hominids and artifacts discovered in Africa. First have them cut out and label poster board shapes to represent the following fossil evidence: bipedal footprints, Lucy, Garhi, *Australopithecus boisei*, *Homo habilis*, Turkana Boy, Turkana Boy's hammerstone, and the flake tool on page 43. Then have them punch a hole in each "fossil" shape and run a length of string through the hole. Now students can suspend the fossils from a wire coat hanger. The oldest fossils should be hung lowest with the others hung at higher intervals.

Tracking Fossils

Have interested students research the location of the actual fossil remains of Lucy, Garhi, and Turkana Boy and make a presentation to the class. The following website provides a listing of locations: *www.pbs.org/wgbh/evolution/humans/humankind/image_credits.html*. As an optional activity, have students choose one of the fossils and write a letter to the museum where the specimen is located to ask questions about it.

ADDITIONAL ASSESSMENT

For Unit 2, divide the class into groups and have them all undertake the Making Footprints project so you can assess their understanding of how paleontologists and archaeologists draw conclusions about ancient hominids based on fossil finds. Use the scoring rubric at the back of this guide to assess students' work, and have students rate their own work with the self-assessment rubric.

LITERATURE CONNECTION

There are numerous enjoyable books that will broaden students' knowledge of early hominids and archaeological exploration. For example:

▶ Johanson, Donald, and Blake Edgar. *From Lucy to Language*. New York: Simon and Schuster, 1996. Nonfiction. Johanson sums up his career in the field and presents a documentary of human life through time on Earth. ADVANCED

▶ Lindsay, William, and Harry Taylor. *Prehistoric Life (Eyewitness Series)*. New York: DK Publishing, 2000. Nonfiction. Captions and a wide variety of illustrations give a broad presentation of prehistoric life on Earth. EASY

▶ McIntosh, Jane. *Archeology (Eyewitness Series)*. New York: DK Publishing, 2000. Nonfiction. This broad, heavily illustrated overview offers a thorough introduction to the field of archaeology. EASY

▶ Walker, Alan, and Pat Shipman. *The Wisdom of the Bones*. New York: Vintage Books, 1997. This account describes the discovery of an intact skeleton of *Homo erectus* in northern Kenya in 1984, and what the find tells us about the day-to-day life of our ancestors. ADVANCED

UNIVERSAL ACCESS

The following activities are designed to cover a range of learning styles and reading, language, and skill levels.

Reading Strategies

▶ There are unfamiliar words in this unit that are not defined in the margins. Have students maintain a classroom word file. Ask one or two students to create word cards for each chapter. On each card, students should write the word, define it, and use it in a sentence. They may add an illustration, if appropriate.

▶ Have partners read sections of the chapters to each other and then ask each other questions about the content, for example: What is the main idea of this passage? What details or examples support the main idea?

Writing Strategies

▶ The painstaking work of archaeological discovery is a subject of several chapters in Unit 2. Invite students to write a list of "dos and don'ts" for participants in an archaeological dig in East Africa. *Dos* might include respecting scientists in charge, being observant, and being willing to withstand harsh conditions and frustration. *Don'ts* could address behavior at the dig, treatment of ancient fossils, complaints about conditions, and impatience.

▶ Have students make a two-column chart comparing Lucy and Turkana Boy with regard to fossil age, the individual's size, how much of the skeleton was found, where it was found, their brain sizes in relation to each other and to humans.

Listening and Speaking Strategies

▶ Small groups can create a monologue for Kamoya Kimeu in which he speaks about working with Mary Leakey at Olduvai Gorge (Chapter 7) and finding the piece of Turkana Boy's fossilized skull in Turkana, Kenya (Chapter 8). Students should present their live or recorded monologues to the class.

▶ Have students consider the individual fossil primary sources in these chapters (bipedal hominid, Lucy, Garhi, Boisei, and Turkana Boy). Ask them to imagine what one of these individuals might express if he or she could communicate to us from millions of years ago. Have students work in pairs to create an interview with one of the hominids—one student asking questions, the other acting as a translator who can interpret the hominid's "language" of grunts, screeches, and gestures.

UNIT VOCABULARY LIST

The following words that appear in Unit 2 are important for your students' understanding of the social studies content as well as for development of literacy. Use these words for vocabulary study or to reinforce language arts skills (e.g., synonyms, compound words, prefixes and suffixes, and related words). Words are listed in the order in which they appear in each chapter.

Chapter 4	Chapter 5	Chapter 6	Chapter 7	Chapter 8
tuff	monotonous	enclosure	ceremonial	putrefying
carcass	anxious	slivers	sideswipe	orientation
	primitive	fracture	excavate	adolescent
	dilemma		strut	pelvis
	paleoanthropologist		marrow	abdomen
			foraging	

A WALK ON THE WILD SIDE: BIPEDS STEP OUT   PAGES 32–35

CAST OF CHARACTERS

Mary Leakey English archaeologist who uncovered early hominid footprints at Laetoli

THEN and NOW

When excavations ended, the site at Laetoli was reburied so that the ancient bipedal footprints would be preserved. But scientists worried that the roots of new vegetation would damage the footprints and between 1995 and 1996, they reopened the site. Most of the footprints were in good condition. After making more accurate contour maps of the tracks, they buried them again. Have a class discussion to talk about why this procedure is important to archaeologists.

CHAPTER SUMMARY

When 3.5-million-year-old evidence of bipedal hominids was found in Africa, scholars were surprised. The discovery led to questions about why our prehistoric ancestors came down from the trees and began to walk on two legs.

PERFORMANCE OBJECTIVES

▶ To explain how fossil footprints were uncovered and analyzed
▶ To understand the importance of bipedalism to hominid development
▶ To describe hypotheses about why some hominids first walked upright

BUILDING BACKGROUND

Ask students if they have heard the expression "Stand on your own two feet." Elicit its meaning. (*Don't rely on others to help you; do things for yourself.*) Ask: Why is "standing on your own two feet" important in our culture? (*It shows independence and self-reliance.*) Explain that in this chapter students will be reading about hominids who walked upright, "on their own two feet," in Africa 3.5 million years ago.

WORKING WITH PRIMARY SOURCES

Review with students how researchers know that the hominid footprints found in Laetoli are more than 3.5 million years old. (Remind students of the information in Chapter 2 on how volcanic eruptions help archaeologists date fossils.) Help students recognize that researchers cannot believe the authenticity of a primary source without proving it.

GEOGRAPHY CONNECTION

Interaction   To help them better understand the preservation of the fossilized footprints found at Laetoli, have students diagram the layers of volcanic tuff and label the diagram with explanations of the volcanic processes that preserve the animal and hominid footprints.

READING COMPREHENSION QUESTIONS

1. What important evidence about hominids was found at Laetoli? (*Footprints showed that bipedal hominids walked upright more than 3.5 million years ago.*)
2. What other footprints besides those of hominids were discovered at Laetoli? (*those of insects, birds, elephants, and a three-toed horse*)
3. How were the footprints made and preserved? (*The footprints were made when animals and insects walked through volcanic ash. The forms of the footprints were baked dry by the sun and were ultimately covered with volcanic ash that hardened and preserved them.*)
4. Distribute copies of the blackline master for Chapter 4. Have students read the information and answer the related questions.

CRITICAL THINKING QUESTIONS

1. What are some of the advantages of walking upright? (*You can carry things in your hands or arms, move faster than on all fours, reach higher than on all fours, and have more of your body exposed to cooling winds.*)

2. How do human spines differ from chimpanzee spines? (*Humans' long spines curve, allowing us to balance on two feet; chimpanzees' spines thrust their heads forward; for balance they stand with their feet wide apart.*)

3. According to some scientists, hominids first stood up in trees. Why? (*Hominids might have stood on tree branches while eating.*)

SOCIAL SCIENCES

Science, Technology, and Society   Have small groups find more information on how archaeologists date fossils and other evidence of prehistoric life. They can go to *http://archaeology.about.com/cs/datingtechniques/a/timing.htm* to begin their search. Each group should report on one of the methods: how it works, the range of dates it can determine, its accuracy, and any drawbacks.

READING AND LANGUAGE ARTS

Reading Nonfiction   Have students read aloud the description of how the Laetoli footprints were preserved. Have students identify the words used to indicate steps in the process (*then, and then, the sequence repeated, gradually, until*). Challenge students to describe in writing a simple process using connecting words like *then* and *next*.

Using Language   Draw students' attention to the word *tuff* and have them distinguish it from the word *tough*. What do the two have in common besides being homonyms? Talk about other English words ending in *-ough* and list some ways we pronounce these words in English. (Examples include *enough, rough, bough, plough, though,* and *through.*)

SUPPORTING LEARNING

Struggling Readers   Have students make a two-column chart contrasting how apes and humans walk, based on information in the text and on the blackline master for Chapter 4.

EXTENDING LEARNING

Enrichment   Students can investigate theories that climate change played a role in hominids becoming bipeds. A good summary appears in "The Transforming Leap, From Four Legs to Two," by John Noble Wilford at *www.pbs.org/wgbh/evolution/library/07/1/text_pop/l_071_04.html*. Have students explain the theories to the rest of the class.

Extension   Have students read the information in the chapter and on the blackline master about how humans and apes walk. Then have them experiment in class, analyzing the way their feet move when they walk normally and when they attempt to walk like an ape.

WRITING

Narrative Have students write a narrative answering the question at the end of the chapter: "Imagine yourself living like our earliest ancestors millions of years ago in the forest or woodland. What would make you stand up?"

LINKING DISCIPLINES

Health Have students investigate the benefits of good posture and the proper way to walk to maximize the benefits of walking for fitness. Ask students to present their findings to the class and to demonstrate good posture and proper fitness walking.

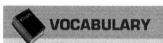

VOCABULARY

bipeds animals that walk on two legs

COMPARING FOOTSTEPS

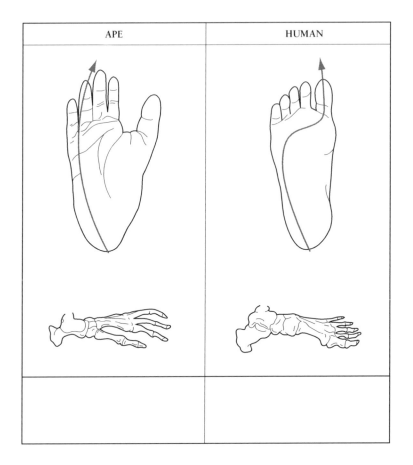

Directions

Read the text below. Based on the illustrations, decide which statements describe humans and which describe apes. Put the letter of each statement in the box under the drawing it describes. Some statements may apply to both.

Statements—Taking a Step

A. Weight is transmitted from the heel.

B. Weight is transmitted along the outside of the foot.

C. Weight is transmitted across the ball of the foot.

D. Weight is transmitted through the middle toes.

E. Weight is transmitted through the big toe.

Statements—Foot Bones

F. The foot has an arch.

G. Toe bones are long relative to feet.

H. Toe bones are short relative to feet.

I. The foot rests flat on the ground.

A. MULTIPLE CHOICE

Circle the letter of the best answer for each question.

1. Which of the following is **not** a hypothesis about why hominids started walking on two legs?
    a. They stood on branches to eat in trees.
    b. They could scavenge food more easily.
    c. They could stand tall and scare off enemies.
    d. They wanted to dance.

2. The name "Footprint Tuff" refers to which of the following?
    a. the person who uncovered the footprints at Laetoli
    b. the difficulty of uncovering the Laetoli footprints
    c. layers of volcanic material covering the Laetoli footprints
    d. the nickname for Mary Leakey

3. Finish this sentence with information from the chapter: One day, 3.6 million years ago, three hominids
    a. went for a walk in the mud.   **c.** died in the mud.
    b. hunted animals in the mud.   **d.** stood in the mud.

4. The evidence at Laetoli settled which of these scientific arguments?
    a. how footprints were preserved for so long
    b. why hominids came down from the trees
    c. which developed first—a big brain or walking upright
    d. when hominids started hunting

5. Which of the following was **not** an animal footprint found preserved at Laetoli?
    a. birds' tracks   **c.** ancient elephant footprint
    b. insect trail   **d.** horseshoe crab trail

B. SHORT ANSWER

Write one or two sentences to answer each question.

6. Why can't monkeys and apes walk on two legs for a long period of time?

7. What sets humans apart from other animals that are bipeds?

8. What are some of the ideas about why hominids started walking on two feet?

C. ESSAY

On a separate sheet of paper, write your own story about the hominids who left their footprints in the mud at Laetoli. Where were they going? What did they see? Why were they going for a walk?

CHAPTER 5

LUCY: THE FAMILY BUSH: MORE HOMINIDS
PAGES 36–41

CAST OF CHARACTERS

Donald Johanson American paleoanthropologist

Lucy *Australopithecus afarensis* (ahs-trul-o-PITH-eh-kus a-far-EN-sis) a 3.2-million-year-old fossilized skeleton found in Ethiopia by Donald Johanson

Tim White American professor who found and described many important hominid fossils

Australopithecus garhi (ahs-trul-o-PITH-eh-kus GAR-hee) species of hominid (2.5 million years old) found by Tim White and colleagues in Ethiopia

WRITING

Journal Have students imagine and then write an interior monologue for Lucy, in which she thinks about what she wants to eat today. Remind students that Lucy was a vegetarian.

CHAPTER SUMMARY

The chapter describes the discovery of a 3.2-million-year-old fossilized hominid. Named "Lucy," the remains of this short female hominid and others like her gave scientists a new species of hominid. Another species, about 700,000 years younger than Lucy, was found in the same area, confirming scientists' suppositions about dramatic changes in hominids between 3.2 and 2.5 million years ago.

PERFORMANCE OBJECTIVES

▶ To understand the significance of the discoveries of *Australopithecus afarensis* and *Australopithecus garhi*
▶ To identify and describe differences between Lucy and Garhi

BUILDING BACKGROUND

Discuss students' experiences with searching for something lost—a car in a parking lot, a contact lens on a carpet or lawn, a pet in a neighborhood. Ask them to describe how they conducted the search—haphazardly or methodically—and which method worked better. Explain that they will read about how two scientists searched for fossils.

WORKING WITH PRIMARY SOURCES

Two of the primary source images in this chapter show Lucy (pages 38 and 39). In the first image, Lucy's fossilized bones are arranged vertically against a white background. They are the only bones in the picture. In the second image, Lucy's remains are displayed horizontally against a dark background as part of a massive exhibit of skulls and fossils. Ask students which image is more effective at conveying the excitement of the discovery and why.

GEOGRAPHY CONNECTION

Regions Open a world atlas to the map of Africa. Have students locate Ethiopia on this map. Then have them study the topography of Ethiopia to identify the different regions of that country, including the northern desert area where Lucy was found.

READING COMPREHENSION QUESTIONS

1. Why do scientists have to collect fossils as soon as they are revealed by erosion? (*Once they are above ground, fossils can be swept away in rainstorms and lost forever. They can also be trampled by livestock or wild game.*)
2. How many individuals were ultimately found in Hadar? (*13*) What types of individuals were they? (*males, females, infants, and juveniles*)
3. Millions of years ago what was the region like where Lucy was found? What is it like today? (*It was a grassland with lakes; today it is a desert.*)
4. What did scientists think had happened to the individuals found at Hadar? (*that they died in a flash flood*)
5. Distribute copies of the blackline master for Chapter 5. Have students read the information and complete the chart comparing the hominids.

CRITICAL THINKING QUESTIONS

1. Why was Lucy's discovery significant? (*Lucy was the most complete hominid skeleton that had ever been found.*)
2. What kind of information were scientists able to gather about Lucy and Garhi by studying their teeth? (*what they ate: Lucy—seeds, nuts, berries, roots; Garhi—meat*)
3. What choices did Donald Johanson, Lucy's discoverer, have to make regarding what to call her? Why did he decide as he did? (*He had to decide which genus she belonged in and he decided on Australopithecus, our hominid "cousin," because she was too primitive to be called human.*)
4. What was so unexpected about Garhi's discovery? (*that there were hominids living in the region at that time who may have butchered animals*)

SOCIAL SCIENCES

Science, Technology, and Society   Have students do further research into the butchered antelope bones found near *Australopithecus garhi* and what this discovery suggests about the early use of tools. First have them record the evidence from Chapter 5 and then do further research into Garhi's use of hammerstones. *Archaeology* magazine's website is a good source for students' research: *www.archaeology.org/online/news/human.html*. Students can present what they learn to the class.

READING AND LANGUAGE ARTS

Reading Nonfiction   Have students use this chapter to summarize the work of archaeologists, and what part luck plays in their findings.

Using Language   This chapter has a powerful description of Lucy's discovery, made more powerful by the authors' use of the word *crunch*. Have students identify the use of *crunch* in all its forms in the chapter. Ask students to note how the word is used on page 38 in the sentence "The crunch, crunch, crunch underfoot stopped them both" to make a point about the care required for archaeological research.

SUPPORTING LEARNING

English Language Learners   Point out the analogy that the authors use to describe the size of Lucy's head on page 38 (*about the size of a softball*). Have students develop an analogy for the size of *human* heads.

Struggling Readers   Have students create a character web for Lucy. They should place her name in the middle of the web, and surround her name with facts from the chapter.

EXTENDING LEARNING

Enrichment   Students can use print references or Internet sources to learn more about Lucy. An interview with Donald Johanson can be found at *www.bbc. co.uk/science/cavemen/indepth/indepth1.shtml*, and more information about Lucy is available at *www.asu.edu/clas/iho/lucy.html*.

Extension   Read aloud the third paragraph on page 37. Then have students design a plan for a "fossil search" using graph paper with a large grid. They can use letters and numbers for *x* and *y* coordinates and then mark paths that take them back and forth over the grid squares horizontally, vertically, or diagonally. Students can use a different-colored marker for each pass.

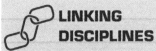

LINKING DISCIPLINES

Arts Bring in a recording of the Beatles song, "Lucy in the Sky with Diamonds" (the name comes from the title of a picture that John Lennon's four-year-old son drew of a classmate named Lucy). Discuss the connection between the song and how hominid Lucy got her name. Then have students write their own verses dedicated to Lucy.

THEN and **NOW**

Donald Johanson discovered Lucy's fossilized skeleton in Ethiopia in 1974. Today Johanson is the director of Arizona State University's Institute of Human Origins.

VOCABULARY

marrow soft fatty material contained in bone cavities

NAME   **DATE**

Directions

Read the newspaper article excerpt below. Use the information in the article and in Chapter 5 to complete the chart comparing Lucy and Garhi.

Skull and Fossils Found in Ethiopia Prompt Missing-Link Debate
by John Noble Wilford
The New York Times, April 23, 1999

Digging beneath a sere plain in Ethiopia, paleontologists have found a skull and other fossils of what they say is a new prehuman species. . . .

Characteristics of the skull, teeth, and limb bones seemed to mark the species as a descendant of *A. afarensis,* which lived from 3.7 million to 3 million years ago and are famously represented by the "Lucy" skeleton from Ethiopia. . . . The *A. garhi* had a projecting apelike face and small braincase, similar to the Lucy species. But its teeth were much larger, which was what most surprised paleontologists about the fossils. . . .

Other skeletal remains at the site included leg and arm bones of what probably, but not certainly, was another member of the new species. From this evidence, scientists said, the individual was slightly less than 5 feet tall and had long legs and a human gait, but long, apelike forearms.

	Lucy	Garhi
Lived	3.2 million years ago	between 2 and 3 million years ago
Height		
Brain size		
Teeth		
Diet		

1. Was "Garhi" truly a surprise to archaeologists? Explain.

_____

2. Which of these hominids, Lucy or Garhi, has characteristics more like a human's? Explain.

_____

NAME   **DATE**

A. MULTIPLE CHOICE

Circle the letter of the best answer to each question.

1. Which of the following is **not** one of the important discoveries about Lucy?
   a. She was a vegetarian.
   b. She butchered antelopes.
   c. She probably ate bugs and snakes.
   d. She was three and a half feet tall.

2. How did Lucy get her name?
   a. It was picked out of a hat.
   b. It was from a popular song.
   c. It was her Ethiopian name.
   d. It was the name of an archaeologist.

3. Choose the statement that best explains why the discovery of 13 individuals in the same place was exciting to archaeologists.
   a. It was the first find of a whole group.
   b. They had died at different times.
   c. They probably died in a flash flood.
   d. They may have known Lucy.

4. Which of the following statements best explains why Donald Johanson named Lucy *Australopithecus afarensis*?
   a. She was a hominid (too primitive to be called human) found in the Afar region.
   b. She was a hominid who had come from afar to the place where she died.
   c. Her fossil skeleton traveled all the way to America, a faraway place.
   d. *Afarensis* means "you are wonderful" in Latin.

5. Which of the following statements best explains why Garhi was a surprise?
   a. No one expected to find a hominid in that area.
   b. The hominid's anatomy and evidence at the site suggests that Garhi used tools and ate meat.
   c. Garhi only ate antelope.
   d. Scientists tripped over his bones.

B. SHORT ANSWER

Write one or two sentences to answer each question.

6. Why does "right time, right place" describe the discovery of Lucy?

7. How do you think Donald Johanson decided to name Lucy *Australopithecus*?

8. What was the significance of finding antelope bones that had cut marks near *Australopithecus garhi* skeletons?

C. ESSAY

On a separate sheet of paper, write an essay explaining this statement: "Garhi was a bipedal primate with a difference."

CAST OF CHARACTERS

Sue Savage-Rumbaugh (SAV-ij-RUM-baw) biologist who studies intelligence of primates

Nicholas Toth American archaeologist and stone tool–making expert

Kanzi (CAN-zee) a bonobo (pygmy chimpanzee) born in captivity in 1980 who has taken part in toolmaking and language experiments

Australopithecus boisei (ahs-trul-o-PITH-eh-kus BOYZ-ee-eye) hominid who lived 1–2 million years ago in East Africa and had large jaws and teeth

Ian Tattersall anthropologist at the American Museum of Natural History and author of many books on human evolution

CHAPTER SUMMARY

Scientists experimented to see whether a modern chimpanzee could chip rocks together to make sharp knifelike stone tools the way toolmaking hominids did in Olduvai Gorge 1.8 million years ago. These prolific hominids made a wide variety of stone tools, as did hominids in Ethiopia 2.5 million years ago.

PERFORMANCE OBJECTIVES

▶ To understand the difference between geofacts and artifacts
▶ To describe the process and purpose of stone knapping
▶ To compare the workmanship of toolmaking hominids to that of a modern bonobo chimpanzee

BUILDING BACKGROUND

Invite students to share their experiences with successfully making something— a model airplane, a cake, a fort from sofa cushions, a skateboard ramp, or an art or craft project. Ask them where they got the materials for their project. Explain that this chapter describes how hominids used the material most widely available to them to make tools.

WORKING WITH PRIMARY SOURCES

Have students consider the image of the 2.3-million-year-old flake tool from Ethiopia on page 43. Ask them to describe what they see. Ask: How big do you think the flake tool is? How do you know? (*The text refers to "fist-sized" rocks.*) Discuss what else could be shown in the picture to give an idea of the tool's size.

GEOGRAPHY CONNECTION

Place Have students read the first paragraph on page 47. Discuss how natural forces such as glaciers and rivers affect rocks—and also affect archaeologists' understanding of excavation sites. Help students understand that a modern scientist has to understand natural forces in order to visualize the environment in a particular place millions of years ago.

READING COMPREHENSION QUESTIONS

1. What was the purpose of the Kanzi experiments? (*to see if a modern bonobo chimpanzee could make tools as well as hominids*)
2. How did the scientists motivate Kanzi to use and make stone-cutting tools? (*They tied a rope around a box containing one of his favorite treats—a juice box— so he would have to cut the rope to get the treat.*)
3. What is the Oldowan Tool Kit, and why did archaeologists give it that name? (*The name refers to the Olduvai Gorge in Africa. So many sliver tools of such a wide variety have been found there that the gorge was likened to a tool kit.*)
4. Why would quartz have been a favorite rock of toolmaking hominids? (*Quartz makes sharp flakes.*)

CRITICAL THINKING QUESTIONS

1. Why do archaeologists think *Australopithecus boisei* might have made tools? (*The hominid's bones have been found at ancient tool sites.*)

2. Compare the stone tools Kanzi made to those hominids at Olduvai Gorge made. (*Kanzi made sharp tools by banging rocks together, but he never showed the control that hominids used to produce stone tools.*)

3. How do archaeologists tell the difference between rock geofacts and artifacts? (*Geofacts often have smoothed edges from millions of years of wear and tear; sometimes archaeologists depend on their knowledge of the site to determine if a rock got there naturally or is an artifact.*)

4. How do we know that hominids did not throw rocks to make tools the way Kanzi did? (*The tools Kanzi made by throwing rocks had random marks, unlike the flaked hominid tools.*)

SOCIAL SCIENCES

Science, Technology, and Society   The experiment to see if a modern bonobo chimpanzee can make tools the way hominids did is an example of using science to understand technology. Have students use information in the chapter to write a paragraph evaluating whether Kanzi's performance as a toolmaker answered the scientists' question on page 42: "Do you think Kanzi could learn to make stone tools the way early humans did?"

READING AND LANGUAGE ARTS

Reading Nonfiction   Have students identify the rhetorical questions posed by the authors on pages 42, 43, and 45–47. (These are not the questions in quotation marks, except on page 42 where a quoted question is answered with a rhetorical one.) Discuss the function of the rhetorical questions—to arouse interest, to organize information, to introduce topics, and to show what questions archaeologists try to answer.

Using Language   Have students note the use of personification in this chapter to describe Kanzi's actions. Discuss how this technique helps show that chimpanzees are relatively close cousins to humans.

SUPPORTING LEARNING

English Language Learners   Have partners discuss the differences between *geofacts* and *artifacts*. Have students point to and name artifacts in the classroom.

Struggling Readers   Distribute the blackline master for Chapter 6 so students can compare Kanzi's toolmaking to that of hominids.

EXTENDING LEARNING

Enrichment   Have students use online souces to find out more about the discovery of 2.5-million-year-old tools at Gona, Ethiopia, and report their findings to the class.

Extension   Ask students to look at the two images of *Australopithecus boisei* and evaluate how effective the artist's reconstruction is. Have them note the skull features they can identify in the reconstruction (heavy brow arches, jutting jaw, cheekbones). Discuss what we can learn from a reconstruction like this.

THEN and **NOW**

Dr. Sue Savage-Rumbaugh, who worked with Kanzi on toolmaking, is now a researcher at the Great Ape Trust of Iowa Research Center, which opened in 2004. Kanzi, born in 1980, is there too.

WRITING

○ **Paraphrase** Have students read the text on page 47 and then write a paragraph explaining in their own words how to tell an ○ artifact from a geofact.

VOCABULARY

Olduvai refers to Olduvai Gorge, a rich archaeological site in East Africa

knap remove flakes from a larger rock by hitting it with a smaller rock

bonobo pygmy chimpanzee

sagittal crest a raised bony ridge running from front to back on top of a skull

geofact something created naturally by the earth

artifact something created by human workmanship

EVALUATING EVIDENCE OF TOOLMAKING

Directions

Read the evidence listed in the left-hand column below and then decide if it is an artifact (something made by humans) or a geofact (something created naturally). Check the correct box, and then explain your reasoning in the right-hand box.

Evidence	Geofact	Artifact	Reasoning
1. battered-looking stone			
2. chiseled-looking stone			
3. stone flakes found with no big rocks nearby			
4. scattered broken stones			
5. sculpted-looking stone			
6. random markings on big rock			
7. knifelike slivers of rock			
8. flaked rocks near what was once a quiet pond			

NAME   **DATE**

A. MULTIPLE CHOICE

Circle the letter of the best answer for each question.

1. Which of the following is **not** a requirement for hominid-style stone knapping?
   a. two rocks or stones
   b. ability to fracture rocks to make sharp flakes
   c. ability to throw one rock at a bigger rock
   d. ability to make stone look sculpted

2. The scientists with Kanzi wanted to find out if Kanzi could
   a. throw stones.   **c.** use a stone tool.
   b. make a stone tool.   **d.** open a juice box.

3. Kanzi's stone tools were not of the same quality as a hominid's because he
   a. couldn't throw stones on the floor.   **c.** wasn't motivated enough.
   b. lacked the control to make flakes.   **d.** was easily distracted.

4. A geofact is an object made by
   a. hominids.
   b. Earth's natural processes.
   c. humans.
   d. factories.

5. *Homo habilis* was given that name because of that species'
   a. clothing.   **c.** interest in hobbies.
   b. toolmaking abilities.   **d.** ability to walk upright.

B. SHORT ANSWER

Write one or two sentences to answer each question.

6. Besides hominid-style knapping, how did Kanzi try to create sharp stone flakes?

   _____

   _____

7. How do scientists know that quartz was prized by early hominids for making tools?

   _____

   _____

8. Why does *Australopithecus boisei* have the nickname "Nutcracker Man"?

   _____

   _____

C. ESSAY

Write an essay on a separate sheet of paper describing the difference between stone tools that were made by hominids and stones that have been shaped by natural processes.

STONES AND BONES: THE OLD STONE AGE

PAGES 48–54

CAST OF CHARACTERS

Kamoya Kimeu (KAM-oy-eh KIM-yew) Kenyan fossil hunter who found many hominids

Mary Leakey English archaeologist who excavated Olduvai Gorge

THEN and NOW

In 1960 Louis and Mary Leakey began to excavate fossils in Olduvai Gorge. Today scientists working with the Tanzanian Department of Antiquities are following in the Leakeys' footsteps, uncovering and preserving Olduvai Gorge fossils.

VOCABULARY

savannah an open plain where tall grasses grow

CHAPTER SUMMARY

At Olduvai Gorge, Mary Leakey made stunning discoveries of 2-million-year-old hominid bones and stone tools, giving rise to a variety of hypotheses about hominid behavior. Assisting Leakey was an extraordinary Kenyan, Kamoya Kimeu, from whose point of view much of the story in this chapter is told.

PERFORMANCE OBJECTIVES

- ▶ To explain the painstaking process of searching for hominid fossils
- ▶ To understand the way fossil evidence is used to reconstruct hominid activity
- ▶ To describe the contributions of workmen like the Kamba at Olduvai Gorge

BUILDING BACKGROUND

Have students look at the picture on page 52. Tell them that the untrained eye sees the people looking at a jumble of bones and rocks. However, the people in the picture, archaeologists and fossil hunters, see a group of hominids sitting around an elephant carcass using stone knives. Tell students that this chapter will reveal how the archaeologists figured this out.

WORKING WITH PRIMARY SOURCES

The image on page 52 shows fossils and artifacts at Olduvai. Discuss how the photograph could be dated using visual clues (style of dress, age of subjects, type of vehicle in background). Then ask students to use visual clues within the photograph to describe the relative size of the extinct elephant bone in the center.

GEOGRAPHY CONNECTION

Regions   Olduvai Gorge is part of the Great Rift Valley, which runs from Syria in the Middle East to Mozambique in southeastern Africa. Have students learn more about this physical feature using print or online resources. Have them draw it on a map and identify the bodies of water that fill parts of the valley.

READING COMPREHENSION QUESTIONS

1. Why was Kamoya Kimeu reluctant at first to take part in the dig at Olduvai Gorge? (*He thought the job was to dig graves, not uncover fossils.*)
2. What did Kimeu conclude about the hominids from examining one of the areas where they ate? (*that they liked to eat antelope; that they ate their food raw*)
3. Why do archaeologists have trouble reconstructing how hominids lived? (*They have so little evidence and the evidence they do have can be interpreted in different ways.*)
4. What did scientists discover about butchering an elephant with stone tools? (*It is difficult to cut through the elephant's skin, but once inside hominids could cut the meat easily.*)

CRITICAL THINKING QUESTIONS

1. Why was the 2-million-year-old "living floor," discovered by Mary Leakey in 1960, of such interest to her? (*She wanted to study what was left to determine why hominids had gathered there.*)

2. How did Mary Leakey uncover objects from consolidated volcanic ash? Why was this a controversial method? (*She used lots of water to dissolve the volcanic ash. Water was in such short supply on the site that workers' drinking water was rationed; workers thought she was wasting water.*)

3. How important were Kamba workers like Kimeu to Mary Leakey's success at Olduvai Gorge? (*The workers provided the backbreaking labor, day in and day out, that removed tons of rock and soil so the fossil evidence could be uncovered and analyzed. Some of the workers, like Kimeu, became fossil hunters themselves.*)

4. What are the theories about how hominids used the "bones and stones" area? Which theory do you think is best? (*Campsite; central foraging area, place where dead animal was found; tool storage area; safe place to stop, butcher food, eat, and rest—storage of tools happened over time. Opinions on which theory is best will vary.*)

5. Distribute copies of the blackline master for Chapter 7 so students can learn more about the life of Mary Leakey.

SOCIAL SCIENCES

Science, Technology, and Society   Have students identify some of the tools scientists and workers used at Olduvai Gorge and explain the significance of the invention of the Olduvai pick.

READING AND LANGUAGE ARTS

Using Language   Point out the analogy in the picture caption on page 48. Make sure students understand the significance of comparing Olduvai Gorge to the Grand Canyon. Show students pictures of the Grand Canyon and have them use it in analogies they create.

Reading Nonfiction   Have students determine from whose point of view most of the information on pages 48–53 is presented. (*Kamoya Kimeu's*) Have students rewrite incidents from the chapter from Mary Leakey's point of view.

SUPPORTING LEARNING

Struggling Readers   Have students make a chart showing the different theories that archaeologists have about the Olduvai Gorge "bones and stones" site excavated.

EXTENDING LEARNING

Enrichment   Students can refer to the text and Internet sources to learn how archaeologists today use computer graphics in their work.

Extension   Read aloud from the first paragraph on page 52 through the top of page 53. Use your voice to express the excitement and wonder of this two-million-year-old scene as imagined by Mary Leakey and Kimeu.

WRITING

Letter Have students imagine that the photograph of Olduvai Gorge on page 48 is a large postcard. Ask them to write a two-paragraph message on the back of the postcard, describing some of the discoveries made there in 1960.

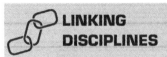

LINKING DISCIPLINES

Health Point out the information about bone marrow on page 52 and have students research and report on the role of fat in digesting protein. They should consider how to correct the idea that all fat is nutritionally "bad."

NAME   DATE

THE LIFE OF MARY LEAKEY

Directions

Read the timeline of Mary Leakey's life, and then answer the questions.

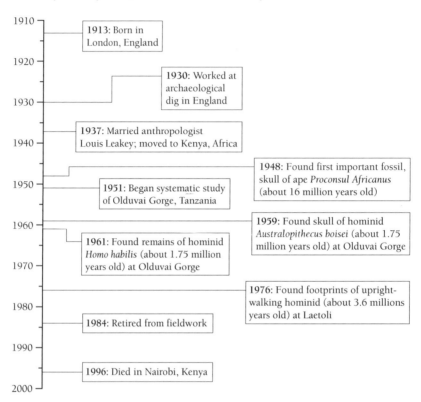

1910

1913: Born in London, England

1920

1930: Worked at archaeological dig in England

1930

1937: Married anthropologist Louis Leakey; moved to Kenya, Africa

1940

1948: Found first important fossil, skull of ape *Proconsul Africanus* (about 16 million years old)

1950

1951: Began systematic study of Olduvai Gorge, Tanzania

1960

1959: Found skull of hominid *Australopithecus boisei* (about 1.75 million years old) at Olduvai Gorge

1961: Found remains of hominid *Homo habilis* (about 1.75 million years old) at Olduvai Gorge

1970

1976: Found footprints of upright-walking hominid (about 3.6 millions years old) at Laetoli

1980

1984: Retired from fieldwork

1990

1996: Died in Nairobi, Kenya

2000

1. How old was Mary Leakey when she first started working on an archaeological dig? Where was that dig?

_____

2. How old was the first important fossil that Leakey found? What was its name?

_____

3. How many years passed between the start of her systematic study of Olduvai Gorge and her first important discovery there?

_____

4. What was the name of the first hominid she found evidence for at Olduvai Gorge?

_____

5. Leakey once commented that her discovery at Laetoli was the most exciting one. Why do you think she would have said this?

_____

_____

NAME   DATE

A. MULTIPLE CHOICE

Circle the letter of the best answer for each question.

1. Olduvai Gorge is called the "Grand Canyon of prehistory" for all the following reasons **except**
   a. it is deep and very beautiful.
   b. many types of evidence have been preserved there.
   c. the evidence there goes back millions of years.
   d. many important discoveries have been made there.

2. The Olduvai pick is the name of
   a. a guitar pick used at Olduvai.
   b. a power shovel used at Olduvai.
   c. a sharp tool invented by the Kamba.
   d. a needle the Kamba use for sewing.

3. Some of the Kamba made fun of Mary Leakey, but Kamoya Kimeu
   a. knew that he could learn from her.
   b. was afraid of her.
   c. argued with her.
   d. taught her how to dig carefully.

4. The "living floor" refers to
   a. the area where the Kamba lived at Olduvai.
   b. a recent layer near the surface of Olduvai Gorge.
   c. a layer 2 million years old and 20 feet below ground at Olduvai.
   d. a section of Mary Leakey's tent.

5. Fossil fever strikes people at archaeological sites such as Olduvai Gorge when they
   a. are bitten by a snake.
   b. stay out in the hot sun.
   c. become allergic to fossils.
   d. develop a strong interest in fossil hunting.

B. SHORT ANSWER

Write one or two sentences to answer each question.

6. How do archaeologists interpret a site to reconstruct a picture of how ancient hominids lived?

_____

_____

7. Why didn't Mary Leakey allow the Kamba workers to sing while they were digging?

_____

_____

8. Why did archaeologists stop calling hominid campsites "home bases"?

_____

C. ESSAY

On a separate sheet of paper, write an essay summarizing the experiences at Olduvai that transformed Kamoya Kimeu into an enthusiastic fossil hunter.

CHAPTER 8

FINDING FABULOUS FOSSILS: TURKANA BOY

PAGES 55–59

CAST OF CHARACTERS

Richard Leakey son of Louis and Mary Leakey, a Kenyan who organizes paleoanthropological expeditions in Kenya

Alan Walker British-born anatomist and paleontologist who has examined many hominids found in East Africa

Turkana Boy (tur-KAHN-a) 1.6-million-year-old skeleton of *Homo erectus* boy found in Kenya

Kamoya Kimeu (KAM-oy-eh) (KIM-yew) Kenyan fossil hunter who found Turkana Boy

Homo erectus (HOE-moe ee-RECT-us) 1.8–.2 million years ago; first hominid to leave Africa; an ancestor to later humans

Meave Leakey paleontologist who has described many East African fossils; wife of Richard Leakey

CHAPTER SUMMARY

In 1984 Kamoya Kimeu, who had been with Mary Leakey at Olduvai Gorge, discovered fossil remains of *Homo erectus*—Turkana Boy—at another site in East Africa. The chapter tells how anthropologist Alan Walker and others reconstructed an almost complete skeleton of an adolescent boy 1.6 million years after he died.

PERFORMANCE OBJECTIVES

▶ To explain the importance of painstaking work and close observation in archaeological research
▶ To understand the significant differences between Turkana Boy (*Homo erectus*) and modern humans
▶ To describe the importance of the spinal column in activities such as walking, breathing, and talking

BUILDING BACKGROUND

Ask students if they are familiar with Christopher Reeve, who played Superman in the movies before suffering an injury to his spinal cord that left him paralyzed from the neck down. Before his death in 2004 he was a champion of spinal cord research. Explain that in this chapter about the discovery of the skeleton of a 1.6-million-year-old boy, they will come to appreciate the modern human spinal cord.

WORKING WITH PRIMARY SOURCES

Distribute the blackline master for Chapter 8 that summarizes Turkana Boy's discovery in the words of Alan Walker.

GEOGRAPHY CONNECTION

Location   Have students turn to page 12 and locate Lake Turkana on the map of Africa. Ask them to trace a line with their fingers connecting the sites from Laetoli to the Middle Awash Valley. Ask: If you were looking for hominids in other parts of Africa today, where would you look? Students should conclude that places with geological histories similar to the eastern African sites would be good places to dig.

READING COMPREHENSION QUESTIONS

1. How tall was Turkana Boy? (*five feet three*)
2. What happened to Turkana Boy's skeleton over 1.6 million years? (*The bones were broken and scattered, and a tree growing in the skull broke it apart.*)
3. Who were the "hominid gang"? (*Kenyans led by Kimeu who were experienced and successful fossil hunters.*)
4. What did scientists conclude about Turkana Boy's ability to speak? (*His spinal cord was too narrow to carry nerves that control breathing to permit speech, so he could not speak.*)

CRITICAL THINKING QUESTIONS

1. How significant were Kimeu's contributions on this dig? (*He found the first piece of Turkana Boy's skull and identified it as* Homo erectus.)

2. How did Alan Walker know that the skull they found was a boy's? (*The browridges were less developed than an adult* Homo erectus's *would be.*)

3. How did the ability to put jigsaw puzzles together with the pieces upside down help Meave Leakey and Alan Walker work on Turkana Boy's skull? (*They could recognize shapes in the shattered fragments of Turkana Boy's skull and see how they fit together.*)

4. What are some of the advantages that Turkana Boy had in a hot climate? (*Turkana Boy was tall, which exposed more skin to the air. He could sweat to cool off. He had lost much of his body hair and had a nose that cooled and moistened air entering his body. These adaptations allowed him to go out in the hot midday sun.*)

SOCIAL SCIENCES

Science, Technology, and Society   Have students look at the photograph on page 55 and read the explanation of what members of the hominid gang are doing in it (second paragraph, page 57). Discuss what tools and scientific attitudes the workers are using. Draw conclusions about how science and technology come together to advance our knowledge of the past.

READING AND LANGUAGE ARTS

Reading Nonfiction   Have students identify the conclusions that Alan Walker and his team drew from the skeleton of Turkana Boy

Using Language   Read aloud the first two paragraphs of the chapter. Have students identify gripping images in the scene (*lying face down in the shallows, head bobbing; fibula snapped in two; sand-filled, upside-down skull held water; perfect pot to sprout; skull burst apart*). Then have them identify the strong verbs that drive these images.

SUPPORTING LEARNING

English Language Learners   Have students collect adjectives used in the chapter, such as *putrefying, sand-filled, upside-down, wait-a-bit, tiny, wretched, detailed, perfect, hot,* and *spool-shaped*. Have partners define the words from the context and use them in sentences.

Struggling Readers   Have students make a two-column chart to summarize the main differences between Turkana Boy (*Homo erectus*) and a modern human.

EXTENDING LEARNING

Enrichment   Students can use text and Internet sources to investigate theories about *Homo erectus's* language capabilities and report their findings to the class.

Extension   To imitate the process described on page 58, enlarge the photograph of the *Homo erectus* skull on page 56 and make copies for students working in small groups. Students can cut the skull pictures into pieces and mix them up, then see who can fit the skull pieces back together in the fastest time.

 **VOCABULARY**

vertebrae spool-shaped bones that make up the backbone

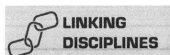 **WRITING**

Process Description Ask students to read the second paragraph on page 57, describing the process that led to Turkana Boy's discovery. Have them write a paragraph describing a "find" of their own, such as cleaning a drawer and finding money, or raking leaves and finding a lost ball.

LINKING DISCIPLINES

Life Science Invite students to read about the human spinal column on page 59. Some can investigate the nerves that control breathing and make speech possible. Others can report on problems caused by spinal cord injuries and breakthroughs in treating them. The group can present its findings to the class.

NAME   **DATE**

INTERVIEWING ALAN WALKER

Directions

The following is a list of questions for an interview with Alan Walker. Locate the answer to each question in the chapter—they all appear as quotations. Summarize the information in each quote and record it in the right-hand column.

Questions	Answers
What did Kimeu tell you about his mood when he found the first skull fragment?	1.
What did you think when you saw that first piece of skull Kimeu found?	2.
When you found pieces of Turkana Boy's skeleton, how did you keep track of what you found?	3.
What led you to believe that Turkana Boy was not an adult?	4.
What makes Turkana Boy a great discovery?	5.
What do you think happened to Turkana Boy after he died?	6.

NAME _____ **DATE** _____

A. MULTIPLE CHOICE

Circle the letter of the best answer for each question.

1. All the following might have happened to Turkana Boy after he died million years ago **except**
   a. he lay face down in water.
   b. he was buried with a ceremony.
   c. animals stepped on his body.
   d. a tree grew out of his skull.

2. The first fossilized piece of Turkana Boy's skull was discovered by
   a. Alan Walker.
   b. Kamoya Kimeu.
   c. the entire "hominid gang."
   d. Richard Leakey.

3. Which statement sums up Alan Walker's opinion of Turkana Boy's value?
   a. For the first time we had an almost complete skeleton to study.
   b. He was too young to be of interest.
   c. The water had damaged his bones so badly we could not analyze them.
   d. We found him in pieces and it was impossible to put him back together.

4. All the following traits helped Turkana Boy stay cool in hot weather **except**
   a. having a nose.
   b. being able to sweat.
   c. being tall.
   d. having a large brain.

5. Vertebrae are
   a. spool-shaped bones in the spinal column.
   b. nerves that control speech.
   c. a way for the body to cool down.
   d. muscles in the chest and abdomen.

B. SHORT ANSWER

Write one or two sentences to answer each question.

6. Why do scientists think that Turkana Boy couldn't talk the way humans can?

_____

_____

7. What were the key factors in finding Turkana Boy?

_____

_____

8. Why was Turkana Boy's nose significant?

_____

_____

C. ESSAY

On a separate sheet of paper, write an essay explaining how observations of Turkana Boy's skeleton allowed scientists to draw conclusions about how _Homo erectus_ lived.

MIGRATING, HUNTING, USING FIRE

PAGES 60–84

UNIT OBJECTIVES

Unit 3 covers from 1.75 million to 90,000 years ago. In this unit, your students will learn

▶ the characteristics of hominid *Homo erectus,* who migrated from Africa leaving fossil evidence from Spain to Indonesia.
▶ how *Homo heidelbergensis* hominids hunted and butchered large animals.
▶ anthropologists' ideas about the nature of Neandertals.
▶ the characteristics of the earliest modern humans.

PRIMARY SOURCES

Unit 3 includes pictures of the following fossils and artifacts:

▶ *Homo erectus* skull, Dmanisi, Republic of Georgia, 1.75 million years ago
▶ Tools, Dmanisi, Republic of Georgia, 1.75 million years ago
▶ *Australopithecus robustus* skull, Swartkrans, South Africa, 1.5 million years ago
▶ Burned animal bones, Swartkrans, South Africa
▶ *Homo antecessor* skull, Gran Dolina, Spain, 800,000 years ago
▶ *Homo antecessor* arm bone with butchering marks, Gran Dolina, Spain, 800,000 years ago
▶ *Homo erectus* skull, Beijing, China, 500,000 years ago
▶ *Homo heidelbergensis* leg bone, Boxgrove, England, 500,000 years ago
▶ Rhino tooth, Boxgrove, England, 500,000 years ago
▶ Hand axe, Boxgrove, England, 500,000 years ago
▶ Tool fragment, Boxgrove, England, 500,000 years ago
▶ Horse bone, Boxgrove, England, 500,000 years ago
▶ *Homo neanderthalensis* skull, Shanidar, Iraq, 50,000 years ago
▶ Flower burial, Shanidar, Iraq, 50,000 years ago
▶ *Homo neanderthalensis* burial, Shanidar, Iraq, 50,000 years ago
▶ *Homo sapiens sapiens* bones, Klasies River Mouth, South Africa, 90,000 years ago
▶ Spear blade, South Africa, 90,000 years ago
▶ Human bones, South Africa, 90,000 years ago

The following excerpts can also be used as primary sources:

▶ Mark Roberts and Michael Pitts, *Fairweather Eden*
▶ Ralph Solecki, *Shanidar*
▶ Ofer Bar-Yosef (Interview)

BIG IDEAS IN UNIT 3

Movement, evolution, and **adaptation** are the big ideas in Unit 3. From the migrations of *homo erectus* to modern humans' control of fire, Unit 3 answers the question of how modern humans evolved. While not all the direct connections have been established, all the hominids discussed in these chapters reveal characteristics that tend toward "human." The roots of human nature are revealed in Unit 3: from *Homo erectus*'s deep-water crossing to reach the Indonesian island of Flores, to the elaborate butchering and burial activities of *Homo heidelbergensis* at Boxgrove, to the burial habits of Neandertals at Shanidar, to the control of fire by *Homo sapiens sapiens* at Klasies River Mouth.

You may want to introduce these ideas by eliciting what students think of as distinctly human characteristics. Point out that these characteristics did not develop suddenly but rather gradually over a long time. Students should understand that hominids coexisted with each other and with modern humans for thousands of years.

GEOGRAPHY CONNECTION

You can refer students to the map on pages 12–13 to locate the sites mentioned in Unit 3. Provide students with an atlas of prehistory showing that England was connected to Europe at the time *Homo heidelbergensis* was starting to hunt large animals (400,000 years ago).

TIMELINE

1.75 million years ago	Hominids live outside Africa at Dmanisi, Georgia
1.5 million years ago	Earliest probable use of fire at Swartkrans, South Africa
800,000 years ago	*Homo erectus* reaches an island in Indonesia by boat
500,000–400,000 years ago	*Homo heidelbergensis* hunts large animals in England; *Homo erectus* lives in China
120,000–70,000 years ago	Early modern humans live at Klasies River Mouth, South Africa

UNIT PROJECTS

Hominid/Modern Human Press Conference

A small group of students can use information in these chapters and other sources to create questions and answers for scripted interviews with *Homo erectus, Homo heidelbergensis,* Neandertals, and *Homo sapiens sapiens.* Questions posed by students acting as reporters should touch on diet, physical appearance, use of tools, and use of fire. The group can present the press conference to the class.

Archaeology Tool Kit

Interested students can investigate how an archaeological dig is organized and what tools and processes archaeologists use to identify, date, and excavate sites such as Boxgrove, Shanidar, or the Klasies River Mouth Cave.

Controlling Fire

Controlling fire to cook food and provide warmth and protection was an important step for modern humans. Have students describe the difference between *using* fire (utilizing fire that occurs randomly in nature) and *controlling* fire (making fire from scratch in order to produce a desired result), and summarize current theories about how humans came to control fire. Students can find this information on the Internet or in encyclopedia entries about fire in prehistory. Students can take the information and develop a skit in which how to control fire is discovered for the first time.

Neandertal Theories

Have students create flashcards using information in Chapter 11 and from other print or Internet sources. On one side of each card they can write one or two sentences describing a theory about Neandertals: for example, that they were gentle or that they could pass among us if dressed in modern clothes. On the other side they can describe the opposing view.

ADDITIONAL ASSESSMENT

For Unit 3, divide the class into groups and have them all undertake the Hominid/Modern Human Press Conference project so you can assess their understanding of the similarities and differences between various hominids. Use the scoring rubric at the back of this guide to assess students' work, and have students rate their own work with the self-assessment rubric.

LITERATURE CONNECTION

There are numerous enjoyable books that will broaden students' knowledge of early humans and evolution, and that they can use for unit projects and other research. Direct students to the following sources as well as to the Further Reading list at the back of the student edition:

▶ Boaz, Noel Thomas, and Russell L. Ciochon. *Dragon Bone Hill: An Ice-Age Saga of Homo Erectus*. New York: Oxford University Press, 2004. Nonfiction. The authors tell about the discovery of the first *Homo erectus* fossils at Dragon Bone Hill in China. They conclude that *Homo erectus* was primarily a scavenger incapable of speech who had learned to tame but not fully control fire. ADVANCED

▶ Peters, Lisa Westberg, and Lauren Stringer. *Our Family Tree: An Evolution Story*. Orlando, FL: Harcourt Children's Books, 2003. Nonfiction. The book uses an illustrated timeline and glossary to give the story of human evolution to young readers. EASY

▶ Tattersall, Ian. *The Last Neanderthal: The Rise, Success, and Mysterious Extinction of Our Closest Human Relatives*. New York: Macmillan General Reference, 1996. Nonfiction. The book provides a thorough investigation of the Neandertals and why they are such an enigma in the story of human evolution. ADVANCED

UNIVERSAL ACCESS

The following strategies are designed to cover a range of learning styles and reading, language, and skill levels.

Reading Strategies

▶ Have students use a K-W-L chart to assist them in their reading. Preview each chapter and have students fill in the first column of the chart with what they *know* about the subject. Have them write what they *want to know* about the subject in the second column. When they are finished with the chapter, have them complete the third column by writing what they *learned*.

▶ Help students organize their understanding of the material by having them outline chapters 9–11 using the hominid names as headings for lists of characteristics. Then as they read about the Klasies people in Chapter 12, they can draw conclusions about the differences between those possibly modern humans and the hominids that preceded them.

▶ Create a class file of unfamiliar words in this unit and their definitions. First have students identify words to be defined. Then ask a group of students to research definitions for the words. Next, write them on index cards and add a sentence using the word correctly. The cards can be made available to the class.

Writing Strategies

▶ Each chapter describes places where important evidence about human evolution has been found. Have students write brief descriptions of each place, organized by continent.

▶ In Chapter 11 a statement by the anthropologist Owen Lovejoy appears at the top of page 80: "The first rule of anthropology is that if everybody believes what you've said, you've probably got it wrong." Invite students to write a paragraph explaining what Lovejoy means, using details from the book about the vagueness of the fossil record.

Listening and Speaking Strategies

▶ To spark student involvement in the material, read the opening paragraph or two of each chapter and have students state their expectations for the chapter.

▶ As you read portions of the chapters, ask volunteers to describe how they imagine different scenes. For example, students may describe the scene when the hominids at Swartkrans Cave "grabbed a burning branch from a grass fire" (page 63) or a Neandertal hunting a large mammal rushed at it with a handheld weapon (page 78). Volunteers could then develop the description into a scene they act out for the class.

UNIT VOCABULARY LIST

The following words that appear in Unit 3 are important for your students' understanding of the social studies content as well as for development of literacy. Use these words for vocabulary study or to reinforce language arts skills (e.g., synonyms, compound words, prefixes and suffixes, and related words). The words are listed below in the order in which they appear in the chapters.

Chapter 9	Chapter 10	Chapter 11	Chapter 12
hulking	ancestry	casual	fainthearted
velociraptor	quarry	displaced	dominance
spotty	flint	mute	revenge
yield	knapper	pollen	
tailing	anvil	sketchy	
restless	Paleolithic	milling stones	
trailblazing		quasi-	
cannibal		niche	
pygmy		mutation	
intentional		disability	
nestled		amputate	
		ritual	
		compacting	
		fleck	

CONNECT THE DOTS: PEOPLING THE GLOBE   PAGES 60–66

FOR HOMEWORK

STUDENT STUDY GUIDE

pages 27–28

CAST OF CHARACTERS

Homo erectus (HOE-moe ee-RECT-us) 1.8–.2 million years ago; first hominid to leave Africa; an ancestor to later humans

Alan Walker British-born anatomist and paleontologist

Ian Tattersall anthropologist and author of many books on human evolution

Alan Thorne Australian paleoanthropologist who studies first Australians

Australopithecus robustus (ahs-trul-o-PITH-eh-kus roh-BUST-us) 1.9–1 million years ago; sturdily built hominid in southern Africa that became extinct

Homo antecessor (HOE-moe ant-ee-SESS-ur) about 780,000 years ago; hominid found in Spain that may be ancestor of Neandertals and possibly modern humans; not universally recognized as its own species

CHAPTER SUMMARY

We know that *Homo erectus* hominids migrated from Africa to other parts of the world, but there is little fossil evidence showing how they got there. The evidence that does exist, in widely separated sites, intrigues scientists who want to know more about these hominids on the move.

PERFORMANCE OBJECTIVES

▶ To describe how *Homo erectus* differed from other hominids and from modern humans
▶ To identify the circumstances that might have caused *Homo erectus* to leave Africa
▶ To understand the clues to *Homo erectus*'s widespread migrations

BUILDING BACKGROUND

Open with a discussion of travel. Ask students to describe places where they have been and where they would like to go. Mark the places on a world map using adhesive notes. Ask the students if they think a desire to travel is a common trait among all the world's people. Explain that in this chapter they will read about hominids who were the world's first long-distance travelers.

WORKING WITH PRIMARY SOURCES

Have students look at the burned animal bones on page 63. Refer them to the chart on page 164 and ask them to locate the date "1.25 million years ago." Reading across the chart they will see that there are two possible hominids who could have used fire in Swartkrans Cave. Have students identify the hominids and discuss the significance of fire use.

GEOGRAPHY CONNECTION

Movement   Copy and distribute the blackline master for Chapter 9. Have students follow the directions for titling the map and annotating it with information about each of the sites where evidence of *Homo erectus*'s migrations has been found. Have them create a legend to explain their markings on the map.

READING COMPREHENSION QUESTIONS

1. What are some of the foods that *Homo erectus* ate? (*meat, roots, berries, shellfish, nuts*)
2. Where was the world's first known barbecue? Why is it important? (*at Swartkrans Cave, South Africa; the first convincing evidence that hominids used fire*)
3. What did scientists find on the Island of Flores that helped change what they knew about hominids? (*Evidence there showed that hominids had crossed deep water long before scientists had previously thought possible.*)
4. How did World War II affect Peking Man? (*Fossils of Peking Man's bones disappeared in the chaos of war in China.*)

CRITICAL THINKING QUESTIONS

1. How do changes in diet help explain the migration of *Homo erectus* from Africa? (Homo erectus *ate all sorts of foods: meat, seeds, berries, and plants. This meant that this species was not tied to one type of plant and so could roam farther from home. Meat also gave* Homo erectus *a high-energy food source, essential for a large brain as well as for migration.*)

2. How does growth in brain size help explain the migration of *Homo erectus*? (*A larger brain meant that* Homo erectus *could adapt better to the differing circumstances of new environments, such as changes in climate and food sources.*)

3. Why was the discovery of *Australopithecus robustus* bones at Swartkrans Cave important? (*It showed that hominids who were not related coexisted and that human evolution did not follow a straight line; rather, there were numerous branches of hominids.*)

SOCIAL SCIENCES

Science, Technology, and Society   Read aloud the statement on page 65, "New environments require new methods to survive." Have students find evidence in the chapter about methods that *Homo erectus* used to adapt to new conditions.

READING AND LANGUAGE ARTS

Reading Nonfiction   Point out the five clues to the migration of *Homo erectus* introduced in this chapter. Ask: What is the connection between clues and the chapter's title? How do the clues help readers understand the chapter's content? Have students work in pairs to identify the questions that each clue raised.

Using Language   Explain that *stride* (page 60, third paragraph) can be a verb or a noun. Reinforce understanding of the word by measuring students' strides. Have each student take ten normal-length strides, then measure the distance covered. Divide that distance by ten to find the length of an individual stride.

SUPPORTING LEARNING

Struggling Readers   Have students make a chart using each of the clues on pages 61–65 as headings and then listing the discoveries at each site.

EXTENDING LEARNING

Enrichment   Students can use Internet sources to discover recent research into the use of fire at Swartkrans Cave. One source is *http://news.bbc.co.uk/1/hi/sci/tech/3557077.stm*.

Extension   Have students study the string grid on page 62, which was used by archaeologists at Swartkrans Cave. Students can create a small-scale version and use it to identify the locations of things at different levels in the classroom.

 VOCABULARY

Homo erectus "upright man"; oldest species of hominid found outside Africa

Australopithecus robustus "robust southern ape"; hominid that lived alongside *Homo erectus* in southern Africa 1–2 million years ago

fire earliest control of fire, 400,000 years ago; earlier fires could have started by lightning

antecessor "one who goes before"

 **LINKING DISCIPLINES**

Science Have students use print and Internet sources to investigate and report on the formation of limestone caves, such as Swartkrans Cave in South Africa or Gran Dolina in Spain.

WRITING

Narrative Have students write a short story about the trip hominids took across deep water to Flores, Indonesia, 800,000 years ago.

NAME   **DATE**

MAPPING THE WORLD OF *HOMO ERECTUS*

Directions

The map shows the locations of the five clues about the migration of *Homo erectus* discussed in the chapter. For each location, write the age of the evidence found there as well as a short description of the evidence.

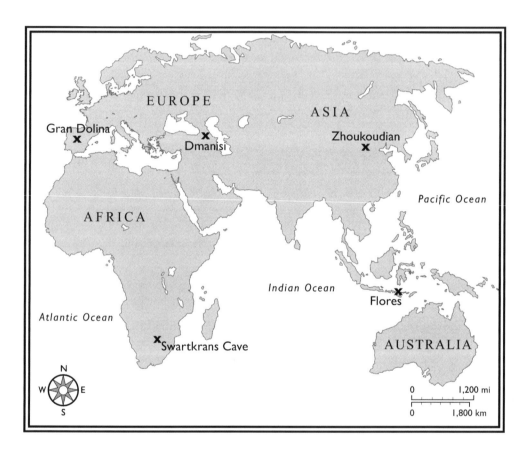

Dmanisi _____

_____

Swartkrans Cave _____

_____

Gran Dolina _____

_____

Flores _____

_____

Zhoukoudian _____

_____

NAME   DATE

A. MULTIPLE CHOICE

Circle the letter of the best answer for each question.

1. Which of the following is **not** a way that *Homo erectus* could have reached Flores, Indonesia?
   a. made a raft   **c.** floated on a tree branch
   b. walked   **d.** swam

2. One reason that *Homo erectus* was able to migrate out of Africa was
   a. a long-legged stride.   **c.** the invention of shoes.
   b. the invention of the wheel. **d.** fear of fire.

3. Which of the following was **not** one of the challenges that *Homo erectus* faced in migrating from Africa?
   a. new climates   **c.** new landscapes
   b. new foods   **d.** new languages

4. What food provided the high energy that *Homo erectus*'s big brain needed?
   a. meat   **c.** roots
   b. plants   **d.** berries

5. In South Africa *Homo erectus* lived alongside which other hominid?
   a. *Homo sapiens*   **c.** Peking man
   b. *Homo antecessor*   **d.** *Australopithecus robustus*

B. SHORT ANSWER

Write one or two sentences to answer each question.

6. Why do scientists think that *Homo erectus* migrated out of Africa?

   _____

   _____

7. What do researchers think about hominids' use of fire at Swartkrans Cave?

   _____

   _____

8. How did scientists date the tools found in Flores, Indonesia?

   _____

   _____

C. ESSAY

Write an essay on a separate sheet of paper detailing the spread of *Homo erectus* from Africa. Include dates and locations from the chapter.

ONCE UPON A RHINO TOOTH . . . : THE STORY OF HUNTING

PAGES 67–72

CAST OF CHARACTERS

Homo heidelbergensis
(HOE-moe HIGH-del-bur-GEN-sis) about 800,000–200,000 years ago; large-brained ancestor of Neandertals and modern humans; found in Europe and Africa

Simon Parfitt British archaeologist in charge of examining animal bones from the Boxgrove, England, site

Mark Roberts English archaeologist, director of the excavations at Boxgrove

 VOCABULARY

Ice Age long period of time when ice covers much of the world's surface

knapper person who knocks rocks together to make stone flake tools

CHAPTER SUMMARY

Excavations at the Boxgrove site in England revealed that *Homo heidelbergensis,* who lived there 500,000 years ago, used sophisticated tools and hunted large animals, including rhinos.

PERFORMANCE OBJECTIVES

▶ To understand the characteristics of *Homo heidelbergensis* at Boxgrove
▶ To describe how scientists established a date for hominid life at Boxgrove
▶ To identify the significance of the Boxgrove site to archaeologists

BUILDING BACKGROUND

Elicit from students what a butcher does and where they have seen butchers work. (*cut up meat; in butcher shops and grocery stores*) Explain that butchers today use modern power tools and steel knives, but their craft is an ancient one. Tell students that in this chapter they will meet the world's first butchers.

WORKING WITH PRIMARY SOURCES

With students, read the craftsman's comment about the Boxgrove hominids' ax-making ability on page 70, and the quotation from Mark Roberts about finding 500,000-year-old hand axes at Boxgrove. Have students explain how this information fleshes out their understanding of *Homo heidelbergensis.*

GEOGRAPHY CONNECTION

Location On a map of Europe, have students find Heidelberg, where *Homo heidelbergensis* was first discovered, and Schöningen, where wooden spears dating back 400,000 to 300,000 years were found. Point out the Boxgrove site, near Chichester on the southern coast of England. Tell students that half a million years ago, England was connected to Europe by land. Discuss how this might strengthen the connection between the hunting hominids of England and Germany.

READING COMPREHENSION QUESTIONS

1. What animals roamed England 500,000 years ago? What was unusual about them? (*Animals we think of as African—rhinos, elephants, and lions—roamed England. They were much bigger than those animals are today.*)
2. What was the main activity at the Boxgrove site? How do we know? (*butchering large animals; from the bones and tools found undisturbed there*)
3. Why did scientists conclude that the Boxgrove hominids did not cook meat? (*There was no evidence of fire.*)
4. What evidence found at Boxgrove showed that these hominids hunted the animals they butchered? (*A hole in a horse's shoulder bone was made by something that had been thrown, like a spear.*)

CRITICAL THINKING QUESTIONS

1. What did the rhino tooth prove about Boxgrove? How? (*Since that species of rhino died out in England before the Anglian ice age began 480,000 years ago, it proved that hominids—whose hand axes were found in the same layer as the rhino tooth—were in England at that time, too.*)

2. Explain how scientists knew the hominid leg bone found at Boxgrove came from a male. (*Based on the size of the leg bone, scientists could tell that the hominid was six feet tall. If a female hominid were that tall, males, who were always larger, would have been giants—very unlikely.*)

3. How is excavating Boxgrove different from excavating a site that has been flooded? (*Things were just as they had been left; nothing was jumbled as fossils can be in sites that have been flooded.*)

4. Mark Roberts believes that something gave the Boxgrove hominids an advantage over the animals at the site. What do you think that advantage was? Support your answer with details from the chapter. (*Some students may suggest that the ability to talk was such an advantage; others may suggest that the use of weapons was the advantage.*)

SOCIAL SCIENCES

Science, Technology, and Society   Discuss speculation in the chapter about whether the Boxgrove hominids talked while they worked. Elicit students' ideas of what they might have needed or wanted to talk about. Ask: Does using tools require speech?

READING AND LANGUAGE ARTS

Reading Nonfiction   Direct students to the following statements in the chapter: "The leg bone found at Boxgrove must have come from a male" (page 68); "These were not dim-witted hominids" (page 70); "The meat would have been eaten raw" (page 71); "The hominids hunted" (page 72). Then have them identify the evidence given to support these statements.

Using Language   Identify similes in the text, for example, *It's like chess* (page 70); *Boxgrove looked as if it were under a spell* (page 70). Have students explain the images that these similes pack into a few words.

SUPPORTING LEARNING

English Language Learners   Make sure students understand the references to fairy tales. The title and first sentence are variations on the traditional fairy tale opening, "Once upon a time." On page 70, Mark Roberts refers to a "spell" and compares Boxgrove to Sleeping Beauty's castle. Have students describe fairy tales that they know.

Struggling Readers   Distribute copies of the blackline master for Chapter 10 so students can review information in the chapter.

EXTENDING LEARNING

Enrichment   Have students investigate possible reasons why the remains of 32 *Homo heidelbergensis* individuals were found together in a pit in a cave near Atapuerca, Spain. One useful source is *http://news.bbc.co.uk/1/hi/sci/tech/3725241.stm.*

Extension   Have students look at the pictures of the rhino skull and tooth on page 68. Discuss the way in which the photographer established the size of the tooth and the skull. Then discuss the significance of the rhino tooth.

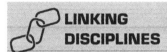

WRITING

○ **Persuasion** Have students write a letter to the editor of the London *Times* supporting the recently announced ○ continuation of excavations at the Boxgrove site and presenting three reasons why they believe it should ○ continue.

LINKING DISCIPLINES

Arts Enlarge the image of the cave bear skeleton on page 70 and distribute copies to students. Ask them to reconstruct how the cave bear might have looked by adding fur and eyes.

THEN and NOW

Digging at Boxgrove has started again. The site was purchased by English Heritage, an organization dedicated to caring for historic sites in England. Students can visit the Boxgrove Projects home page at *http://www.ucl.ac.uk/boxgrove.*

HOMO HEIDELBERGENSIS AT BOXGROVE

Directions

Review the picture of *Homo heidelbergensis* hominids butchering a horse at Boxgrove. Then answer the questions.

1. What are figures 2 and 3 doing? _____

2. Figure 6 is kneeling to do his work. What do you think he is making and how complicated is the job?

_____

3. Figure 1 is pointing to something in the distance, possibly an animal coming to chase the hominids away from the horse carcass. Based on what you know about Boxgrove, what animal might be in sight?

_____

4. Why are figures 4 and 5 on guard? How will they sound the alarm? _____

5. Why might hominids 1, 4, and 5, and 2 and 3 need to communicate with each other? Do you think

they did? How? _____

A. MULTIPLE CHOICE

Circle the letter of the best answer to each question.

1. Compared to modern human adults, *Homo heidelbergensis* was
   a. about the same size.   c. much smaller.
   b. much larger.   d. child-sized.

2. Which of the following is **not** a reason that the rhino tooth and skull were important finds at Boxgrove?
   a. The tooth made it possible to date the site to 480,000 years ago.
   b. The tooth's age proved that hominids were in England before the Anglian ice age.
   c. The tooth indicated that rhinos in England suffered from tooth decay.
   d. The skull indicated that hominids at Boxgrove did not cook their food.

3. The Paleolithic (Old Stone Age) period lasted from 2.5 million years ago until
   a. about 1 million years ago.   c. about 10,000 years ago.
   b. about 100,000 years ago.   d. the present.

4. Which one of these animals was found buried with hominid adults and children in a cave in Spain?
   a. cave bear   c. sabretooth cat
   b. Tyrannosaurus rex   d. horse

5. Why did scientists have to be careful handling the hand axes that they uncovered at Boxgrove?
   a. They were still as sharp as the day they were made.
   b. They were jumbled together with other fossil evidence.
   c. They could break easily.
   d. They were buried in lava.

B. SHORT ANSWER

Write one or two sentences to answer each question.

6. What evidence convinced scientists that hominids at Boxgrove hunted the animals they butchered?

   _____

   _____

7. What is the condition of the finds at Boxgrove?

   _____

   _____

8. Why didn't the Boxgrove hominids seem to be afraid of dangerous beasts?

   _____

   _____

C. ESSAY

Boxgrove's hominids can be called *hunters*, *butchers*, and *craftsmen*. On a separate sheet of paper, write an essay explaining why each of these nouns applies to Boxgrove hominids.

WILL THE REAL NEANDERTAL PLEASE STAND UP?   PAGES 73–80

CAST OF CHARACTERS

Neandertal (nee-AND-ur-tahl) about 200,000–29,000 years ago; close relative of modern humans, found in Ice Age Europe and western Asia

Ralph Solecki (sol-ECK-ee) directed excavations at Shanidar Cave in Iraq

Ofer Bar-Yosef archaeologist and professor of anthropology who investigates the origins of agriculture and modern humans

Lewis Binford archaeologist who has studied ancient and modern hunters and gatherers

 VOCABULARY

milling stones stones used to grind grain into flour

compassionate caring for others

CHAPTER SUMMARY

The nature of Neandertals is a subject of debate among anthropologists. Evidence from European and Iraqi sites have given rise to contradictory ideas about Neandertal attributes and abilities. Anthropologists do agree that these hominids used fire and were well adapted to cold weather.

PERFORMANCE OBJECTIVES

▶ To explain how Neandertals differ from us
▶ To understand some of the ways that anthropologists view Neandertals
▶ To describe Neandertals' physical attributes and adaptation to cold

BUILDING BACKGROUND

Invite students to explain the saying, "You can't judge a book by its cover." Discuss the experience of being wrong about someone or something based on a superficial judgment. Explain that this chapter is about a group of hominids who are often misjudged because of their "cover." Then read aloud the description of a Neandertal on page 75 and elicit from students the differences between Neandertals and humans.

WORKING WITH PRIMARY SOURCES

After students read the interview with Ofer Bar-Yosef (pages 76–77), have them evaluate the usefulness of this type of primary source. Ask: What is different about reading the words Bar-Yosef *spoke* rather than the words he *wrote*?

GEOGRAPHY CONNECTION

Location   Copy and distribute the blackline master for Chapter 11. Students will use information (text and map) to draw conclusions about Neandertal sites.

READING COMPREHENSION QUESTIONS

1. What did the discovery of flowers in a Neandertal burial site suggest to anthropologist Ralph Solecki? (*that Neanderthals cared about the person who was buried there*)
2. Based on evidence found by Ralph Solecki, what was wrong with Nandy? How did other Neandertals treat him? (*Nandy had a withered arm and was blind. He was supported by other Neandertals.*)
3. How did the Neandertals' hunting methods affect their bodies? (*They suffered many injuries from rushing in close to stab large mammals.*)
4. How do scientists know that Neandertals used fire in Shanidar Cave? (*Hearths were found with charcoal flecks stuck to the stones.*)

CRITICAL THINKING QUESTIONS

1. Why do you think the interview with Ofer Bar-Yosef was included in this chapter? (*Students should understand that the interview gives readers an inside view of what an archaeologist thinks about his work and discoveries.*)
2. Explain how Neandertals were physically well equipped for cold weather. (*Their large noses cooled them off, protecting them from the risk of overheating, and therefore sweating, in frigid weather.*)
3. On page 80, the authors write, "There is always the danger we see only what we want to see. . . . " How does that statement relate to the dispute over what Neandertals were like? (*People who prefer to see Neandertals as gentle—or beastly—interpret evidence to suit their preferences.*)
4. In your opinion, which anthropologist—Solecki, Bar-Yosef, or Binford— presents the most convincing argument about Neandertals' nature? (*Answers will vary.*)

SOCIAL SCIENCES

Science, Technology, and Society   Read the sidebar on page 78 with students and discuss how physical evidence of Neandertal injuries led scientists to speculate about the weapons and methods Neandertals used for hunting. Interested students can investigate the tools and methods used in forensic anthropology and report back to the class.

READING AND LANGUAGE ARTS

Reading Nonfiction   Have volunteers read the Archaeologist at Work feature (pages 76–77) aloud with you. Have the students ask the questions, and you give the answers. Elicit from students how a feature like this one adds to the text.

Using Language   Remind students that despite differing opinions about Neandertals' nature, anthropologists agree on their physical description. Have students examine the first paragraph on page 75, from "The Neandertal's face" to "built for abuse." Then ask them to identify the simile as well as nouns, adjectives, and verbs used to describe Neandertals in this paragraph.

SUPPORTING LEARNING

English Language Learners   Retell the fairy tale "Beauty and the Beast" so students can better understand the contradictory interpretations of Neandertals in the chapter.

Struggling Readers   Have students make a three-column chart headed *Solecki, Binford,* and *Bar-Yosef.* Have them summarize each anthropologist's views on the question posed in the chapter subtitle: Neandertal—Beauty or the Beast?

EXTENDING LEARNING

Enrichment   Students can use online sources to learn more about Ofer Bar-Yosef's excavations and conclusions. One site that contains both technical and easily understood information is *http://antiquity.ac.uk/ProjGall/Adler/adler.html.*

Extension   Read the dramatic opening paragraph of the chapter aloud and discuss the fact that when modern-day scientists experienced an earthquake they were able to understand the injuries suffered by Neandertals who had lived in the same cave 50,000 years earlier.

THEN and **NOW**

In March 2004 the *Smithsonian Magazine* reported that one of the nine Neandertal skeletons Ralph Solecki found in Shanidar Cave is in the Smithsonian's National Museum of Natural History along with copies of the eight other skeletons. The original eight skeletons remained in Iraq and are now presumed lost.

WRITING

Narrative Invite students to write a short story about Nandy, the Neandertal who had a disability and was looked after by other Neandertals. Students should base the story on the anthropologist Ralph Solecki's conclusions in the chapter.

LINKING DISCIPLINES

Health Review how Neandertal bodies dealt with cold (page 79). Have students investigate how humans can be affected by hypothermia and how people in cold climates can protect themselves.

SOME MAJOR NEANDERTAL SITES

Directions

Use the information on the map about Neandertal sites to answer the questions below.

NEANDERTAL SITES IN EUROPE AND ASIA

1. Of these sites, which has the oldest evidence of Neandertals? Which has the most recent evidence?

_____

2. Based on the age of evidence found at these sites, how long did Neandertals live in Croatia? How long did they live in Israel?

_____

3. Evidence from two of the sites shows that Neandertals lived at both places at the same time. Which sites were these?

_____

4. Use the mileage scale to determine how far apart these two sites are.

_____

NAME _____ DATE _____

A. MULTIPLE CHOICE

Circle the letter of the best answer for each question.

1. Which of the following is **not** a physical feature of Neandertals?
  a. chin   **c.** browridges
  b. huge teeth   **d.** sturdy body

2. Neandertals were killed in Shanidar Cave by
  a. wild animals.   **c.** rock falls.
  b. cannibals.   **d.** floods.

3. The saying "You can't judge a book by its cover" applies to Neandertals because
  a. they had big brains but did not use fire.
  b. they looked gentle but acted brutally.
  c. their sturdy bodies did not protect them from the cold.
  d. they look brutish but may have acted tenderly toward each other.

4. One explanation for the injuries suffered by Neandertals is that they
  a. had to fight other hominids.   **c.** were clumsy.
  b. often fought amongst themselves.   **d.** hunted with short thrusting spears.

5. The evidence that Neandertals at Shanidar practiced burial rituals include
  a. flowers and branches in graves.   **c.** burnt sacrifices in the graves.
  b. clothing worn by the deceased.   **d.** tools in the graves.

B. SHORT ANSWER

Write one or two sentences to answer each question.

6. How do scientists know that Neandertals were "built for the cold"?

_____

_____

7. How did Neandertals' facial features differ from those of modern humans?

_____

_____

8. Until how many years ago did Neandertals survive in western Asia?

_____

_____

C. ESSAY

Write an essay on a separate sheet of paper explaining why scientists think that Neandertals mourned their dead. Use details from the comments of Solecki and Bar-Yosef in the chapter to support your main idea.

BRAIN FOOD: THE MIDDLE STONE AGE

PAGES 81–84

CAST OF CHARACTERS

Hilary Deacon archaeologist who has excavated Stone Age sites in southern Africa

Homo sapiens sapiens (HOE-moe SAY-pee-ens) about 150,000 years ago and the present; modern humans; this term means "wise, wise people"

Tim White professor who found and described many important hominid fossils

THEN and NOW

On page 84 the authors write, "Fully modern humans . . . hunt dangerous prey." Discuss with students whether they think that seeking out danger is a modern human characteristic. Talk about extreme sports and television shows where people test themselves against dangers.

CHAPTER SUMMARY

Evidence found at the Klasies River Mouth in South Africa may point to one of the first modern human groups. Their physical characteristics, sophisticated tools, and control of fire set the Klasies people apart from earlier hominids, but there is disagreement about whether their behavior, including cannibalism, was truly human.

PERFORMANCE OBJECTIVES

▶ To describe the lifestyle of the Klasies River Mouth people
▶ To recognize what characteristics distinguish modern humans
▶ To draw conclusions about the Klasies River Mouth people from archaeological evidence

BUILDING BACKGROUND

Elicit from students the behavior (*food-gathering, toolmaking, use of fire, complex belief systems, etc.*) and anatomy of the hominids discussed in the book so far, and have them compare these to the behavior and anatomy of present-day humans. Ask: Can we point to any group of hominids so far that come close to what modern humans are like in behavior and anatomy? Tell students that the archaeological evidence discussed in this chapter may point to a 90,000-year-old modern human group from South Africa.

WORKING WITH PRIMARY SOURCES

Have students look at the picture on page 84 of human bones from the Klasies River Mouth. Read the text on the page, and have students draw conclusions as to why most scientists believe these are modern human bones rather than hominid bones.

GEOGRAPHY CONNECTION

Place The physical features of the Klasies River Mouth site were advantageous to the Klasies people. Have students identify the physical features that provided protection, food, water, and a way of hunting larger animals. (*Students should identify the caves, abundant seafood, river water, and the cliffs over which the people could have driven the herds of eland.*)

READING COMPREHENSION QUESTIONS

1. Why isn't the site at the Klasies River Mouth a place for the fainthearted? (*The people who lived there 100,000 years ago were cannibals.*)
2. Why did Hilary Deacon call Klasies "the oldest seafood restaurant in the world"? (*He found evidence that the people there had cooked shellfish that was readily available along the shoreline.*)
3. What evidence exists that Klasies people were capable of complex thought? (*Their cannibalism may have been ritual; they controlled fire for warmth, cooking, and protection; they crafted varied tools; and they altered their environment.*)
4. What physical details in the bones found at Klasies convinced scientists that they were modern human bones? (*The bones indicated a modern appearance: delicate limb bones, jawbones with chins, and no browridge on the forehead.*)

CRITICAL THINKING QUESTIONS

1. Why were Klasies tools an improvement on tools made by *Homo erectus?* (*Possible answer: The thinner blades meant that Klasies people could cut things better; using blades for spears meant that Klasies people could hunt more efficiently and safely.*)

2. What indirect evidence is presented in the chapter that the cannibalism of the Klasies people was part of a complex belief system? (*The site—on the junction of a river and the ocean—provided abundant seafood. Bones of eland and other animals, as well as remains of plants, show that the people had a varied diet. This indicates that the Klasies people probably had enough food and that their cannibalism was not the result of starvation.*)

SOCIAL SCIENCES

Science, Technology, and Society   Have students look at the spear blade on page 83. Have them consider what changes in the lives of the Klasies people such a technological development caused. Then have them find out more about the definition of technology and draw conclusions about why it is a hallmark of modern humans. Students can use websites such as *www. bergen.org/technology* to gather information.

READING AND LANGUAGE ARTS

Reading Nonfiction   From the last paragraph on page 81 through the second paragraph on page 83, the text talks about the possible reasons for the Klasies people's cannibalism. Have students pick out the main ideas of this section and list the details used to support them.

Using Language   Point out the tongue-in-cheek way that cannibalism is discussed in the quotes from Hilary Deacon (page 81) and Tim White (page 82). Discuss why humor may sometimes be helpful in writing about difficult subjects.

EXTENDING LEARNING

Enrichment   Refer students to the sidebar on page 82 and then have them use Internet and print sources to learn more about the methods scientists use to analyze dirt found at archaeological digs. They can create a poster displaying what they have learned.

Extension   Distribute copies of the blackline master for Chapter 12. Then read the chapter aloud to students and have them use the blackline master to take notes on the evidence for and against the Klasies people being fully modern humans. Students can use their graphic organizers to debate the question.

SUPPORTING LEARNING

English Language Learners   Using the opening paragraph of the chapter, demonstrate to students how to paraphrase. Then have small groups read the chapter to each other section by section while the rest of the group takes notes. Each member of the group should then use his or her notes to paraphrase a section. Encourage group members to help each other with word choice.

Struggling Readers   Have students make a three-column chart with the headings *Klasies People, Chimpanzees,* and *Homo erectus.* While reading the chapter, they can use the chart to take notes on the three categories, concentrating on the differences between them. They can use this information to evaluate whether the Klasies people were truly modern.

 VOCABULARY

cannibal human or animal that eats others of its own species

ritual a formal ceremony, often with religious meaning

easy pickings something that is easy to get or capture

 **WRITING**

Persuasion Are the Klasies River Mouth people fully modern or near modern? Have students write an essay in which they take one side or the other. Students should use direct and indirect evidence as well as theories from the text to support their positions.

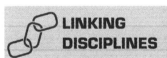 **LINKING DISCIPLINES**

Art Distribute copies of the picture of Klasies Cave on page 82 and have students tape it to a large sheet of drawing paper. Then have them extend the picture beyond the borders of the photograph by surrounding the cave with drawings of details mentioned on page 83.

KLASIES PEOPLE—MODERN HUMANS OR NOT?

Directions

Use details from Chapter 12 to fill in the chart. Then answer the questions using complete sentences.

Category of Evidence	Proof That Klasies People Were Fully Modern	Proof That Klasies People Were Not Fully Modern
Behavior		
Anatomy		

1. Do you believe that the Klasies people were fully modern humans? Explain your answer.

_____

_____

2. Tell what additional evidence would make you certain that the Klasies people were fully modern. Explain why this would help.

_____

_____

NAME   **DATE**

A. MULTIPLE CHOICE

Circle the letter of the best answer for each question.

1. Scientists can tell that the Klasies people practiced cannibalism by
  a. the tools found there.
  b. the marks on human bones there.
  c. the lack of other food there.
  d. the size of the fires used there.

2. Ritual cannibalism is a sign of modern behavior because it is proof of
  a. cooking skills.
  b. killing skills.
  c. war-like behavior.
  d. a complex belief system.

3. Which of the following was **not** a feature of the Klasies site?
  a. desert
  b. cliffs
  c. ocean
  d. cave

4. Which of these foods did Klasies people hunt with spears?
  a. shellfish
  b. mastodon
  c. eland
  d. plants

5. Which of the following is evidence that Klasies people were modern humans?
  a. They looked like us.
  b. They hunted.
  c. They cooked.
  d. They lived in a cave.

B. SHORT ANSWER

Write one or two sentences to answer each question.

6. How do the bones of Klasies people support the idea that they were modern humans?

_____

_____

7. What advantage does a blade attached to a spear give to a hunter?

_____

_____

8. What are some of the things people can do when they control fire?

_____

_____

C. ESSAY

Use information from the chapter to write an essay on a separate sheet of paper supporting the idea that the Klasies people were modern humans. Include references to fire, bones, cannibalism, and tools.

ON OUR WAY: MODERN HUMANS EMERGE

PAGES 85–104

UNIT OBJECTIVES

Unit 4covers a period from about 45,000 to 24,500 years ago. In this unit, your students will learn about the surge in creativity and technological innovation that marked the Cro-Magnons' emergence in Europe and will consider the Neandertals' disappearance. Through an evocative Dreamtime story, they will discover beliefs about how people came to Australia and what the fossil evidence reveals about the same period. In this unit, your students will learn

▶ theories about what happened to the Neandertals and how modern humans (Cro-Magnons) came to dominate Europe.

▶ Aboriginal stories and archaeological evidence related to peoples' coming to Australia.

▶ facts about the Cro-Magnons' technological innovations.

▶ theories about the purpose of Cro-Magnon paintings discovered in Chauvet Cave.

PRIMARY SOURCES

Unit 4 includes pictures of artifacts and excerpts from the following primary sources:

▶ *Homo sapiens sapiens* skeleton, Lapedo Valley, Portugal
▶ Pendant, Lapedo Valley, Portugal
▶ Aboriginal Dreamtime story, Australia
▶ Harpoon, Anège, Fance
▶ Clay animals, Dolni Věstonice, Czech Republic
▶ *Homo sapiens sapiens* skeleton, Sunghir, Russia
▶ Cave bear bones, Chauvet Cave, France
▶ Cave bear drawing, Chauvet Cave, France
▶ Hand stencil, Chauvet Cave, France
▶ Fire remains, Chauvet Cave, France
▶ Horse drawing, Chauvet Cave, France
▶ Cave bear skull, Chauvet Cave, France

BIG IDEAS IN UNIT 4

Change and **creativity** are the big ideas presented in Unit 4. The unit discusses changes in Europe starting about 35,000 years ago when Cro-Magnons spread across Europe and the Neandertals began to disappear. It details the creativity of the Aboriginal story describing how humans came to Australia. The unit also presents archaeological evidence confirming details in that story. Finally, it explores the extraordinary changes in Cro-Magnon Europe—from the creativity expressed in technology to the artistry and variety of cave paintings. Introduce these ideas by discussing what students know about times of change in other contexts and how they can lead to creative innovation.

GEOGRAPHY CONNECTION

Refer students to the map on page 12–13 and maps within each chapter. For Chapters 13, 15, and 16, provide an outline map of Europe that shows how far south the ice extended during the period 45,000–25,000 years ago.

TIMELINE

More than 40,000 years ago	People first settle in Australia
32,000 years ago	Paintings and engravings in Chauvet Cave, France
30,000 years ago	People first settle Solomon Islands
27,000 years ago	People build mammoth bone shelters, weave clothing, and make ceramic figures at Dolní Věstonice, Czech Republic
25,000 years ago	The Kid—a Neandertal–modern human hybrid or a modern human child, lives and dies in the Lapedo Valley, Portugal

UNIT PROJECTS

Drama

Invite a group of students to create a skit about the first use of a harpoon or a sewing needle. Working without props, students can act out a conversation in which an inventive Cro-Magnon introduces his or her idea for the new tool to a skeptical group. To expand this project to include the whole class, have one group create a similarly-themed skit about building a hut using mammoth bones, another a skit about dressing a body for burial using ivory beads, and another create a skit about using a kiln to form clay figurines of humans and animals.

Megafauna of Australia

Interested students can research and report on some of the giant animals of Australia that the first humans encountered there. Using information from the Australia Museum website, they can make life-size drawings of creatures like the giant short-faced kangaroo that roamed Australia in the Pleistocene Age: *www .lostkingdoms.com/facts/factsheet51.htm.* (This site gives dimensions in meters.)

Cave Formation

A group of interested students can research the formation of limestone caves like Chauvet Cave in France and then prepare and illustrate an oral presentation. A brief explanation of cave formation can be found at *http://school.discovery.com/ lessonplans/programs/landforms.* Alternatively students can develop a demonstration of cave formation and present it to the class. One suggestion, using clay, water, and sugar cubes, can be found at *www.explorethecaverns.com/lessons/guide1a.html.*

Cave Art

Cover part of a classroom wall with brown butcher paper that has been crumpled to simulate the uneven surface of a cave wall. Provide chalk or charcoal and invite students to trace their hands, copy animal paintings shown in Chapter 16, or copy paintings shown on the Chauvet Cave website: *www.culture.gouv.fr/ culture/arcnat/chauvet/en/index.html.* Students may also draw modern animals.

ADDITIONAL ASSESSMENT

For Unit 4, divide the class into groups and have them all undertake the Drama project so you can assess their understanding of the change that occurred in Paleolithic technology 45,000 years ago and how it affected the life of Cro-Magnons. Use the scoring rubric at the back of this guide to assess students' work, and have students rate their own work with the self-assessment rubric.

LITERATURE CONNECTION

There are numerous enjoyable books that will broaden students' knowledge of Cro-Magnons and Australian Aborigines. For example:

▶ Lauber, Patricia. *Painters of the Caves.* Washington, DC: National Geographic, 1998. Nonfiction. Illustrated with artifacts, photographs, and artwork derived from cave paintings, this book gives an overall picture of daily life for the cave dwellers. AVERAGE

▶ Noonuccal, Oodgeroo, and Bronwyn Bancroft. *Dreamtime: Aboriginal Stories.* New York: HarperCollins, 1994. Fiction. The Dreamtime Aboriginal stories are retold and illustrated in this volume. AVERAGE

UNIVERSAL ACCESS

The following strategies are designed to cover a range of learning styles and reading, language, and skill levels.

Reading Strategies

▶ Have students create charts showing the main ideas and supporting details for each of the chapters in Unit 4.

▶ Have students look in Chapter 13 for answers to the question "What became of the Neandertals?" Ask them to list the answers and add definitions of unfamiliar words to the class's word file.

▶ Call on students to read the opening of each of the chapters in Unit 4. Encourage them to make their voices expressive. Fit the chapter opening to the abilities of each student.

Writing Strategies

▶ Have students write a letter to Jean Clottes, the archaeologist in charge of Chauvet Cave, explaining why they would like to visit the cave. In the letter they should mention specific paintings or fossils in the cave that interest them.

▶ Have students create a catalog of Cro-Magnon tools and jewelry. They can name and describe each item and explain why it is better than anything previously available.

▶ Have students make a comparison–contrast chart for the tools Neandertals and earlier hominids used and those the Cro-Magnons developed.

Listening and Speaking Strategies

▶ Have students create person-in-the-street interviews with Cro-Magnons in Dolní Věstonice. The questioner can ask about uses for mammoth bones.

▶ In a talk-show format, have two student interviewers talk to two student guests playing Chris Stringer and Cidália Duarte. The questions should focus on information in Chapter 13 about the discovery of the Kid, and the theories about what happened to Neandertals.

▶ Invite a group of students to read the Dreamtime story in Chapter 14 aloud.

UNIT VOCABULARY LIST

The following words that appear in Unit 4 are important for your students' understanding of the social studies content as well as for development of literacy. Use these words for vocabulary study or to reinforce language arts skills (e.g., synonyms, compound words, prefixes and suffixes, and related words). The words are listed below in the order in which they appear in the chapters.

Chapter 13	**Chapter 14**	**Chapter 15**	**Chapter 16**
tedious	island-hop	inventory	billowing
pendant	freakishly	crochet hook	parietal
climactic		skittish	prehistoric
caliper		hearth	shaman
protractor		rotisserie	
		kiln	
		figurine	
		tunic	

CAST OF CHARACTERS

Cidália Duarte (SEE-dahl-ee-ah DWAR-tay) Portuguese archaeologist who excavated skeleton of the Kid

The Kid 25,000-year-old skeleton of a child buried in rock shelter in Portugal

Cro-Magnons (CROH-MAN-yon) 35,000–10,000 years ago; the first modern humans in Europe

Christopher Stringer paleontologist at the Natural History Museum in London

CHAPTER SUMMARY

Scientists disagree about why Neandertals disappeared from Europe just as modern humans (Cro-Magnons) started thriving there. A 25,000-year-old fossil skeleton that seems to have both Neandertal and Cro-Magnon features has fueled the debate.

PERFORMANCE OBJECTIVES

▶ To explain the significance of the discovery of the Kid's skeleton
▶ To consider various explanations for the Neandertals' disappearance
▶ To understand the meaning of the expression "We are all Africans"

BUILDING BACKGROUND

Ask students to think about a time when they were passionately interested in a hobby, a sport, or a project to the exclusion of practically everything else. Discuss the feeling of being absorbed in something in which others are not so interested. Offer an example from your own experience and then explain that in this chapter students will be reading about a person who sacrificed a great deal to enlarge our knowledge of Neandertals.

WORKING WITH PRIMARY SOURCES

Students can draw their own conclusions about the physical differences between Cro-Magnons and Neandertals. Pictures of both types of skulls can be found on-line or in print resources. One useful website is *http://news.nationalgeographic.com/news/2003/03/photogalleries/neanderthal*. Have students place the pictures side by side and identify differences.

GEOGRAPHY CONNECTION

Interaction The rock shelter in which the Kid was found was formed by an overhanging cliff. Elicit from students other natural structures that hominids and early humans might have used for shelter. (*caves, fallen trees*)

READING COMPREHENSION QUESTIONS

1. In what modern-day country and in what type of shelter was the Kid found? (*Portugal; a rock shelter under an overhanging cliff*)
2. What was there about the Kid that surprised scientists? (*The Kid seemed to have both Neandertal and Cro-Magnon features.*)
3. What are some of the theories about the Neandertals' disappearance? (*They were massacred by Cro-Magnons, were killed by diseases spread by Cro-Magnons, gradually faded out because the Cro-Magnon population grew more rapidly, or blended into Cro-Magnons through intermixing.*)
4. One theory about early modern humans is that they moved into Europe from Africa. What is the other theory? (*that they evolved from existing populations, such as Neandertals*)

CRITICAL THINKING QUESTIONS

1. Which theory about modern humans—"Out of Africa" or evolution from other populations—do you think is stronger? Why? (*Answers will vary. Students should support their opinions with details from the chapter and their own research.*)

2. Read the New Meaning to the Term "Gym Rat" sidebar on page 87. Does this prove anything about the differences in bones between Neandertals and modern humans? Why or why not? (*Answers will vary.*)

SOCIAL SCIENCES

Science, Technology, and Society   Ask students to examine the picture of the pendant on page 86. Point out that this is the first picture of prehistoric jewelry in the book. Have students draw conclusions about the people who might have made such an artifact. (*Possible answers: These people had skills to make the pendant as well as the desire and time to make something meant for ornamentation. These people were like modern humans in some ways.*)

READING AND LANGUAGE ARTS

Reading Nonfiction   Read the quotation from Chris Stringer at the bottom of page 89. Have students write a paragraph interpreting this part of the statement: "Human differences are mostly superficial. What unites us is far more significant than what divides us."

Using Language   Reread with students the first two pages of the chapter, and identify the mood of tenderness created by the authors. Have students find words and phrases that produce this mood.

SUPPORTING LEARNING

English Language Learners   Have partners make a list of the nouns in this chapter that name tools scientists use. Students can write the nouns, their definitions, and a sentence using the noun on note cards and add the cards to the class's word file.

Struggling Readers   Distribute copies of the blackline master for Chapter 13. Have students complete the chart comparing the theories about the Neandertals' disappearance.

EXTENDING LEARNING

Enrichment   Invite interested students to use the following Internet source to define mitochondrial DNA (mtDNA) and learn about the results of experiments comparing Neandertal and modern European mtDNA: *www.pbs.org/wgbh/nova/ neanderthals/mtdna.html*.

Extension   Using the picture of a skull on page 88 as a reference, have students locate the places on the skull that Chris Stringer mentions in the text directly above the photograph: skull height, breadth, and width; angle of forehead; projection of browridge.

WRITING

News Article Have students write a news article reporting on either Cidália Duarte's work on the Kid's skeleton or Chris Stringer's mission to measure fossil skulls. Students should conduct additional research to answer the who? what? when? where? why? questions and may include opinions of other scientists in their articles.

LINKING DISCIPLINES

Art Have students trace the shell pendant on page 86 and then transfer it to a piece of cardboard. They can then cut it out, color it red, and hang it on a piece of string or ribbon.

THEN and NOW

Chris Stringer recently reported that the Kid's upper front teeth and inner ear are being analyzed for evidence of Neandertal or modern features. Stringer suggests that since Portugal was very cold 25,000 years ago, perhaps the Kid's Neandertal features were simply a sign of modern humans adapting to the cold.

NAME   DATE

WHY NEANDERTALS DISAPPEARED

Directions

The chart below has been completely filled in with one theory about the Neandertals' disappearance. Complete the rest of the chart with information from the chapter about other theories.

Event	Theory	Cro-Magnons	Neandertals	Result for Neandertals
Climate grows colder; big animals disappear	A	Adapt hunting methods to new conditions	Do not adapt hunting methods	Die out from starvation
Cro-Magnons come in contact with Neandertals	B			Gradually evolve into modern humans
	C	Massacre Neandertals		
	D		Have no immunity, so get sick and die	
	E	Push Neandertals away from places where they can hunt		

1. Which of these theories does Chris Stringer's research contradict?

_____

2. Which of these theories (if any) do you find plausible? Why?

_____

NAME   DATE

A. MULTIPLE CHOICE

Circle the letter of the best answer for each question.

1. How old was the Kid when he died?
  a. 2   **c.** 8
  b. 4   **d.** 14

2. Which of these objects did Cidália Duarte find with the Kid's skeleton?
  a. wooden doll   **c.** shell pendant
  b. bone flute   **d.** cave bear skeleton

3. The Kid caused a stir in the scientific community because
  a. no Cro-Magnons had been found in Portugal before.
  b. of the way he was buried.
  c. he seemed to be part Cro-Magnon and part Neandertal.
  d. he was wearing jewelry.

4. Which of the following is **not** a theory about why Neandertals died out?
  a. They intermixed with Cro-Magnons.
  b. They died of diseases spread by Cro-Magnons.
  c. They were massacred by Cro-Magnons.
  d. They froze to death in the Ice Age.

5. According to Chris Stringer, Neandertals
  a. definitely intermixed with early modern humans.
  b. are not the ancestors of modern humans.
  c. died out gradually.
  d. died out suddenly.

B. SHORT ANSWER

Write one or two sentences to answer each question.

6. What was unusual about the Kid's features?

_____

_____

7. What research did Chris Stringer do before coming to his conclusions about Neandertals?

_____

_____

8. Some scientists do not support the Out of Africa theory of the evolution of modern humans. What do they believe instead?

_____

_____

C. ESSAY

On a separate sheet of paper, write an essay explaining the evidence that supports Neandertals being ancestors of modern humans. Identify which piece of evidence you think is most important.

DUCK HUNTING— RUN! THE PEOPLING OF AUSTRALIA

PAGES 90–92

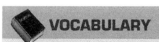

VOCABULARY

megafauna all the large animals found in one area, such as Australia

CHAPTER SUMMARY

An ancient Aboriginal story describes how the first people came to Australia. Scientists are tantalized by the story's descriptions of a sea voyage and giant animals. The voyage is still a mystery, but the animals' existence has been confirmed by fossil evidence.

PERFORMANCE OBJECTIVES

▶ To understand the Aboriginal story explaining how humans arrived in Australia
▶ To describe the megafauna of prehistoric Australia
▶ To identify the story elements that scientists have confirmed and those that remain a mystery

BUILDING BACKGROUND

Invite students to discuss legends with which they are familiar. These might be legends explaining features of the natural world, such as thunder; larger-than-life heroes like Paul Bunyan; or real-life heroes like George Washington. Explain that in this chapter students will be reading a legend that explains events that occurred over 40,000 years ago.

WORKING WITH PRIMARY SOURCES

Invite a student to read aloud the Dreamtime story excerpt on page 91. Point out that Dreamtime stories were an oral tradition. To illustrate, invite another student to retell the story excerpt. Then have a third student retell it. Discuss the differences in the three versions. Consider the way an oral tradition shapes stories over thousands of years.

GEOGRAPHY CONNECTION

Place   One interpretation of the Dreamtime story suggests that the earliest people came to Australia via "an island pathway" from Southeast Asia. Distribute the blackline master for Chapter 14 so students can learn more about Pleistocene coastlines.

READING COMPREHENSION QUESTIONS

1. In the Dreamtime story, what is Whale's role? Why is he angry at the end of the story? (*Whale's canoe was used for the journey to Australia; at the end of the trip Bird accidentally punched two holes in the canoe and it sank, making Whale angry.*)

2. What is Starfish's role in the story? (*Starfish distracts Whale so others can steal his canoe; he ends up in a fight with Whale and punches a hole in Whale's head that can be seen today.*)

3. What evidence supports that people used boats to reach Australia? (*People used boats 30,000 years ago to reach the Solomon Islands, which are near Australia.*)

4. How was the Dreamtime story passed from generation to generation? (*People were told the story and in turn told it to their children.*)

CRITICAL THINKING QUESTIONS

1. Why is it significant that obsidian can be found throughout the Solomon Islands? (*Since obsidian occurs in only a few places in the Solomon Islands, finding it throughout the islands means that the people who lived there traded among themselves and traveled back and forth among the islands.*)

2. Why will it be difficult to find evidence of the first people to come to Australia? (*They probably settled along the coast in areas that are now under water.*)

SOCIAL SCIENCES

Economics   Have students use encyclopedias to find out more about obsidian, a rare, highly valued stone used in trade among Pacific islanders. Pose these questions: What is obsidian? Why might it have been highly prized? What is the connection between the appearance of obsidian on certain islands and the theory that people traded with it?

READING AND LANGUAGE ARTS

Reading Nonfiction   Point out that although the chapter is built around a Dreamtime story, it contains much factual information about the peopling of Australia. Have students evaluate the way that the story and facts are connected in the chapter. Ask: Do the facts intrude on the story? Does the story make it harder to grasp the facts? What would be another way to present both the facts and the story in a single chapter?

Using Language   Have students note the use of italics and capital letters in the text. (See pages 90 and 92.) Call on volunteers to read these sentences aloud to show how the typestyle adds emphasis.

SUPPORTING LEARNING

Struggling Readers   Have students categorize the information from the Dreamtime story and the factual research by using a two-column chart labeled *Dreamtime Story* and *Evidence*. They can list the story's key points in the first column and the fossil evidence that confirms the story's content in the second column.

EXTENDING LEARNING

Enrichment   Students can visit the website of Australia's Wonambi Fossil Centre and use the information they find there to prepare a presentation about Australian megafauna: *www.environment.sa.gov.au/parks/naracoorte/wonambi/index.html*.

Extension   Have partners find pictures of modern versions of the animals named on page 92—wombat, kangaroo, tortoise, snake, lizard, and duck—as well as the creatures from the Dreamtime story—whale, koala, and starfish.

WRITING

- Have students write a dialogue between two humans who encounter the "Demon duck of doom" (page 91) or
- another giant animal when they first come ashore in Australia.

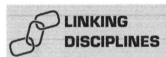

LINKING DISCIPLINES

Art Have students choose a scene from the Dreamtime story and illustrate it in comic-book style (with speech bubbles) or in a style of their choosing.

NAME   **DATE**

OCEAN TRAVEL IN THE PLEISTOCENE AGE

Directions

Study the map, then answer the questions below.

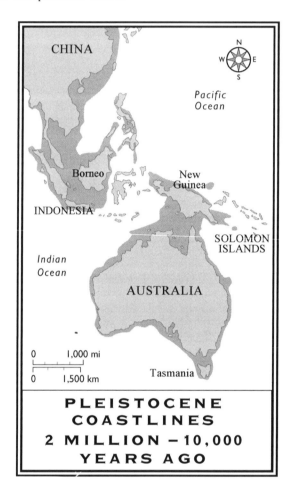

1. In the Pleistocene Age, what islands were connected to Australia? What islands were connected to China?

   _____

2. If ancient people had traveled from what is now China directly to Australia, what is the shortest distance they would have had to travel over water?

   _____

3. What is the shortest distance from ancient Indonesia to ancient Australia?

   _____

4. Trace a possible route from China to Australia by traveling overland and "island-hopping." Calculate how far the trip is. Calculate the longest distance over water.

   _____

NAME   DATE

A. MULTIPLE CHOICE

Circle the letter of the best answer for each question.

1. Which is **not** a way the earliest people might have reached Australia?
   a. island-hopping from Indonesia
   b. walking all the way from China
   c. traveling by boat from the Solomon Islands
   d. traveling by land and by boat from China

2. The "Demon ducks of doom" were Australian
   a. comic book characters.   **c.** science experiments gone wrong.
   b. movie characters.   **d.** megafauna.

3. Which of these statements describes the Dreamtime story?
   a. an Aboriginal story about their origins
   b. the plot of an Australian TV show
   c. a description of megafauna
   d. a typical Australian bedtime story

4. The following animals live in Australia today
   a. wallabies   **c.** snakes that are three feet around
   b. giant ducks   **d.** ten-foot-tall lizards

5. Why were the animals that the first Australians faced when they arrived so unusual?
   a. They were a combination from many different lands.
   b. They were tame.
   c. They attacked the humans as well as other animals.
   d. They had evolved in isolation for millions of years.

B. SHORT ANSWER

Write one or two sentences to answer each question.

6. What elements in the Dreamtime story about Whale probably indicate the truth?

_____

_____

7. How do scientists account for the disappearance of Australian megafauna?

_____

_____

8. What does the presence of ancient obsidian tools on many of the Solomon Islands tell us about the early people of that region?

_____

_____

C. ESSAY

Write an essay on a sseparate sheet of paper explaining the truths that are buried in the Dreamtime tale retold in this chapter.

CHAPTER 15

ON THE WAY TO THE MALL: COMPLEX PALEOLITHIC TECHNOLOGY

PAGES 93–97

CAST OF CHARACTERS

Cro-Magnons (CROH-MAN-yon) 35,000–10,000 years ago; the first modern humans in Europe

THEN and **NOW**

Globalization means that people on every continent now have or want the same "stuff." American-style blue jeans, shirts with sports logos, music videos, and sodas are found in Bali, Belize, and Beijing, as well as Berlin, Burundi, and Brasilia.

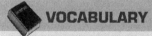 **VOCABULARY**

mammoth a very large, hairy, elephant-like mammal that became extinct during the last ice age

CHAPTER SUMMARY

About 45,000 years ago, in a burst of creativity, Cro-Magnons started using new materials to make and improve tools. They invented new arts such as bead making. This flowering of technology sets Cro-Magnons apart from other people in prehistory and raises the question "Why did it happen?"

PERFORMANCE OBJECTIVES

▶ To identify and describe Cro-Magnon innovations in tools, arts, and hunting methods
▶ To explain how these new tools and new materials were improvements over the old ways of doing things
▶ To understand the debate about the reasons for Cro-Magnon advances in technology

BUILDING BACKGROUND

Discuss the chapter title with students. Elicit connections between Paleolithic technology and "the mall" as they know it. Ask: What evidence of toys, clothes, jewelry, and cooking utensils have they read about so far in the book? (*none, except for the Kid's pendant in Chapter 14*) Ask students to predict what this chapter will contain.

WORKING WITH PRIMARY SOURCES

Have students look at the photograph on page 95 and answer the following question: What does this picture suggest to you about why Cro-Magnons came to Dolní Věstonice? (*Possible answer: The piled-up bones suggest the remains of a mammoth hunt or a structure built with the bones.*)

GEOGRAPHY CONNECTION

Place Have students read the Regional Differences sidebar on page 93. Elicit regional differences found in the United States today. Discuss what caused regional differences during the Paleolithic Age. (*types of animals available, other resources, climate, and so on*)

READING COMPREHENSION QUESTIONS

1. What were some of the new materials Cro-Magnons used for tools? (*antlers, bones, ivory*)
2. What new hunting methods did Cro-Magnons develop? (*hunting with nets; fishing*)
3. Why do archaeologists think the Cro-Magnons came to Dolní Věstonice? (*to gather bones of mammoths who had died there*)
4. What is one explanation for the 10,000 beads found with a skeleton at Sunghir in Russia? (*The beads were sewn onto clothing that has since disintegrated.*)

CRITICAL THINKING QUESTIONS

1. How did their new tools change Cro-Magnons' life? (*The new tools made life easier and safer. Cro-Magnons could throw lighter spears at dangerous animals rather than having to attack at close range. Axes with handles could chop wood faster. Fishhooks and sewing needles made fishing and sewing more efficient.*)

2. Why do the authors compare the burst of creativity 45,000 years ago to the spread of modern shopping malls? (*Cro-Magnons went from having very few tools to having many and varied tools. This makes them seem more like modern-day humans, who have thousands of products to choose from.*)

SOCIAL SCIENCES

Science, Technology, and Society   Have students consider how technological developments contributed to Cro-Magnon society. For example, how did access to mammoth bones and the construction of strong mammoth-bone fences and huts affect the lifestyle of Dolní Věstonice's people?

READING AND LANGUAGE ARTS

Reading Nonfiction   Distribute copies of the blackline master for Chapter 15 so students can organize ideas about new and improved Cro-Magnon technology. Help students understand the cause-and-effect relationship of technology and human behavior.

Using Language   Point out that the information in the chapter is organized as answers to one main question on page 93—"When did everything change on Earth?"—and several follow-up questions. Have students locate the answers to the main question and identify the follow-up questions and answers.

SUPPORTING LEARNING

English Language Learners   Explain to students that the word *mammoth*, which is the name of a now-extinct living creature, is also an adjective. Students can define the adjective, use it in a sentence, and add it to the class's word file.

Struggling Readers   Have students use the Outline graphic organizer at the back of this book to summarize the information in the chapter.

EXTENDING LEARNING

Enrichment   Interested students can learn more about recent mammoth research in Siberia using the American Museum of Natural History website: *www.amnh.org/exhibitions/expeditions/siberia.* Have them report their findings to the class.

Extension   Have interested students make clay copies of the animals shown on page 96. Ask them to name their animal, write a label describing it, and display it in class.

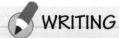

WRITING

Persuasion Have small groups create ads promoting the use of one of the "new and improved" Cro-Magnon tools. The ad should explain how the tool can benefit its users.

LINKING DISCIPLINES

Health Some scientists have linked Cro-Magnon creativity to the use of language. Have interested students investigate recent scientific research on the development of language at *www. newscientist.com/ news/news.jsp? id=ns99996303.*

NAME   DATE

CRO-MAGNON TOOLS AND TECHNOLOGY

Directions

Use information in the chapter to complete the chart, explaining how each Cro-Magnon development might have changed the way people lived.

Tool or Technology	Lifestyle Change
Barbed spear point	
Spear-thrower	
Beads	
Building with mammoth bones	
Axe with handle	
Sewing needle	
Net	

NAME _____ DATE _____

A. MULTIPLE CHOICE

Circle the letter of the best answer for each question.

1. Before 45,000 years ago, most artifacts found at archaeological sites were directly related to
   a. survival.   **c.** religion.
   b. art.   **d.** superstition.

2. Which of the following was **not** a tool developed by Cro-Magnons?
   a. spear-thrower   **c.** wheelbarrow
   b. sewing needle   **d.** hunting net

3. Mammoth bones were used for all the following except
   a. food.   **c.** fuel.
   b. fences.   **d.** needles.

4. What is the significance of the ivory beads found buried with the skeleton in Russia?
   a. Early humans used beads as currency.
   b. The person buried with the beads was a woman.
   c. The beads were stolen.
   d. Humans were starting to make objects for rituals and personal adornment.

5. Which of the following is a possible reason for Cro-Magnons' burst of creativity?
   a. use of language   **c.** influence of Neandertals
   b. smaller brain   **d.** sudden desire for "cool stuff"

B. SHORT ANSWER

Write one or two sentences to answer each question.

6. How does adding a handle to a tool improve the tool?

   _____

   _____

7. Why did Cro-Magnons come to the site of Dolni Véstonice?

   _____

   _____

8. How do you think advances in technology affected the lives of Cro-Magnons?

   _____

   _____

C. ESSAY

This chapter describes the Cro-Magnons as *creative*. On a separate sheet of paper, write an essay naming areas in their lives in which they were creative. Support your ideas with details from the chapter.

CRAWLING THROUGH CAVES: ROCK ART

PAGES 98–104

FOR HOMEWORK

STUDENT STUDY GUIDE

pages 41–42

THEN and NOW

Chauvet Cave is now owned by the French government. To minimize biological exchanges with the outside world, people who enter the cave wear protective clothing and shoes that never leave the cave. Inside, special monitors track the temperature and other conditions to make sure the artwork is not damaged. Have students write a short paragraph telling why such precautions are important.

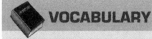 **VOCABULARY**

Paleolithic: *Paleos + lithos* = "old" + "stone"; Old Stone Age, archaeologists' term for period from first stone tools to the end of the last ice age

CHAPTER SUMMARY

The walls of Chauvet Cave in southern France—discovered by chance by three cave-diving friends in 1994—reveal the vibrant work of Cro-Magnon artists who painted by firelight 32,000 years ago.

PERFORMANCE OBJECTIVES

▶ To explain how Chauvet Cave was discovered
▶ To understand why the art in Chauvet Cave is unique
▶ To describe in detail how artists worked in Chauvet Cave

BUILDING BACKGROUND

Ask students if any of them has explored a cave or cavern. Discuss the appeal of this type of exploration while pointing out the hazards of caving. Invite interested students to find out about local caves or caverns and report back to the class.

WORKING WITH PRIMARY SOURCES

Have students choose one of the cave paintings shown in the chapter and describe its impression on them orally or in writing. If possible, provide a book with color pictures of Chauvet Cave paintings, such as Patricia Lauber's *Painters of the Caves.*

GEOGRAPHY CONNECTION

Place   The chapter says that Chauvet Cave is a limestone cave. Have students investigate why many caves are found in areas where there are layers of limestone underground. Students can make and display diagrams showing how limestone caves are formed.

READING COMPREHENSION QUESTIONS

1. What did three French cave explorers discover by chance in 1994? (*a cave containing 32,000-year-old cave paintings*)
2. What was the cave used for 32,000 years ago? (*No one knows for sure, but they do know that no one lived there.*)
3. The explorers used headlamps to see; what did the artists 32,000 years ago use for light? (*They lit fires and held torches.*)
4. What colors were used by the artists in Chauvet Cave? (*red, black, and yellow*)

CRITICAL THINKING QUESTIONS

1. How can you tell that the paintings in Chauvet Cave are much more than just simple drawings? (*The authors describe the paintings as complex works that show great skill.*)

2. Look at the picture of the horse on page 103. How did the artists use the claw scratches in the painting? (*The scratches were incorporated as the legs and lower body of the horse.*)

3. Why do you suppose Paleolithic artists would climb into cold, damp, dark caves to draw their pictures? (*Answers will vary.*)

SOCIAL SCIENCES

Science, Technology, and Society   Have students investigate the methods used to protect the paintings in Chauvet Cave from the humans who visit the cave. They can refer to information on the Chauvet Cave website.

READING AND LANGUAGE ARTS

Reading Nonfiction   Distribute copies of the blackline master for Chapter 16, and have students compare and contrast Chauvet Cave and Lascaux Cave.

Using Language   Have students look through the chapter for words related to exploring caves. List the verbs and positional words attached to them: climb *down*, crawl *in*. Make a list of those words and add words not in the chapter but also related to exploring caves.

SUPPORTING LEARNING

Struggling Readers   Invite students to act out the discovery of the cave paintings in Chauvet Cave, specifically, Chauvet climbing down into the darkness (page 100); Deschamps's discovery of the first painting when her headlamp shone on it (page 101); and all three explorers discovering handprints (page 102) and having their headlamps start to dim.

EXTENDING LEARNING

Enrichment   Students can use print and Internet sources to learn more about the techniques the artists used at Chauvet and why the art discovered there is unique. They can visit the Chauvet Cave website for information and a virtual tour: *www.culture.gouv.fr/culture/arcnat/chauvet/en/index.html.*

Extension   This chapter features a dramatic story of discovery. Have students take turns reading aloud the paragraphs on pages 98–102. Model an expressive tone of reading for students to imitate.

WRITING

○ **Narrative** Have students choose one of the cave paintings mentioned in the chapter—the cave bear, handprint, or
○ horse—and write a short story about the artist telling what it was like entering the cave, lighting a fire, being among cave
○ bear bones, and creating the work.

LINKING DISCIPLINES

Art Invite students to find out what specialists have to say about the Chauvet Cave paintings by visiting the Witnesses section of the Chauvet Cave website (*http://www.culture. gouv.fr/culture/arcnat/ chauvet/en/index.html*) or using print resources. In the Witnesses section, scholars from many different fields who have been allowed to enter the cave comment on the art they saw there. Students can choose one or two of these accounts to read and report on.

COMPARING THE LASCAUX AND CHAUVET CAVES

Like Chauvet Cave, Lascaux Cave contains Ice Age art. But Lascaux is a very different site, containing much more recent art than is found at Chauvet. In the 1940s and 1950s many thousands of people visited the cave at Lascaux, damaging the art on the walls. Lascaux is now open only to researchers.

Directions

Complete the chart with information about Chauvet Cave from the chapter.

	Chauvet Cave	**Lascaux Cave**
Country		France
When discovered		September 1940
Discovered by		Four teenage friends who were exploring
Age of paintings		17,000 years old
Subjects of paintings		Prehistoric animals: aurochs, deer, horses, cows, wild goat, cave lions
Evidence of lighting		Stone lamps that burned oil
Evidence of people		Handprint of five-year-old child; oil lamps; fossilized rope
Visits to cave	Closed to all except researchers who apply for permission to spend time in cave. Never open to the public.	Open to the public from 1948 to 1963. Closed to all except a limited number of researchers since 1963 to protect paintings. Lascaux II, a replica, opened to the public in 1984.
Virtual tour of cave	*www.culture.gouv.fr/culture/ arcnat/chauvet/en/index.html*	*www.culture.gouv.fr/culture/ arcnat/lascaux/en*

1. How are Chauvet and Lascaux Caves similar?

_____

2. How old were the cave paintings at Chauvet when Lascaux painters were just starting?

_____

3. What do you consider the most important difference between the two caves? Why?

_____

NAME _____ **DATE** _____

A. MULTIPLE CHOICE

Circle the letter of the best answer to each question.

1. Which of the following was **not** found in Chauvet Cave?
   a. cave bear bones
   b. evidence of fires and torches
   c. prehistoric art
   d. evidence of cooking

2. How would you describe the art in Chauvet Cave?
   a. portable
   b. parietal
   c. partly portable
   d. partly parietal

3. What was the cave like when the explorers first entered it in 1994?
   a. brightly lit by fires
   b. pitch black
   c. lit by sunlight
   d. lit by moonlight

4. Besides pictures of animals, Chauvet Cave contains pictures of
   a. buildings and tools.
   b. families.
   c. hands and symbols.
   d. religious rituals.

5. The pictures in Chauvet Cave are different from art in other caves because the animals were
   a. all alive at the time.
   b. hunted animals.
   c. tame animals.
   d. dangerous animals.

B. SHORT ANSWER

Write one or two sentences to answer each question.

6. Why did scientists decide that prehistoric humans did not live in Chauvet Cave?

   _____

   _____

7. Why did the three discoverers of Chauvet Cave feel as if they would meet the Cro-Magnon artists?

   _____

   _____

8. What kinds of techniques did the artists of Chauvet Cave use?

   _____

   _____

C. ESSAY

Put yourself in the place of one of the discoverers of Chauvet Cave. On a separate sheet of paper, write an essay telling about your feelings as you first enter the cave, when you drop down into the large room, and when you first see the paintings.

MOVING ON, SETTLING DOWN
PAGES 105–130

UNIT OBJECTIVES

Unit 5 covers the period from 12,500 years ago to 8,500 years ago. In this unit, your students will learn

▶ theories about how people came to the Americas.
▶ how archaeological evidence at Monte Verde, Chile, challenged long-held beliefs about the origins of humans in the Americas.
▶ the evidence of Ice Age and post–Ice Age life in the Americas found at La Brea and Koster.
▶ where farming and domestication of animals first began.
▶ the mysteries uncovered at Çatalhöyük.

PRIMARY SOURCES

Unit 5 includes pictures of the following artifacts and fossils:

▶ Mastodon bone, Monte Verde, Chile
▶ Stone drill, Monte Verde, Chile
▶ Structure, Monte Verde, Chile
▶ Foundation, Monte Verde, Chile
▶ Plant remains, Monte Verde, Chile
▶ Plant and animal fossils, Los Angeles, California
▶ Dog grave, Koster, Illinois
▶ Bone and clay beads, Koster, Illinois
▶ Hairpins, Koster, Illinois
▶ *Homo sapiens sapiens* toe bones, Abu Hureyra, Syria
▶ *Homo sapiens sapiens* neck bones, Abu Hureyra, Syria
▶ *Homo sapiens sapiens* arm bones, Abu Hureyra, Syria
▶ *Homo sapiens sapiens* teeth, Abu Hureyra, Syria
▶ Flint dagger, Çatalhöyük, Turkey
▶ Houses, Çatalhöyük, Turkey
▶ Mural, Çatalhöyük, Turkey
▶ *Homo sapiens sapiens* skeleton, Çatalhöyük, Turkey
▶ Bricks, Çatalhöyük, Turkey
▶ Obsidian, Çatalhöyük, Turkey

BIG IDEAS IN UNIT 5

Movement, settlement, diversity, and **change** are the big ideas presented in Unit 5. The movement of people from Asia into the Americas is the big move covered in this unit. Monte Verde, Koster, Abu Hureyra, and Çatalhöyük are all examples of settlement, but the sites are so diverse that it is difficult to make generalizations. Another major development is farming. Change is the constant across all these sites.

You can introduce these ideas by discussing students' experiences with moving and settling down. People who move from place to place often want to stay put, whereas those who have always lived in the same place want to travel to new places. Discuss the changes in people's lives brought about by moving on and settling down.

GEOGRAPHY CONNECTION

Refer students to the maps on pages 12–13 and 109. If possible, provide detailed maps showing the prehistoric Bering Land Bridge and the modern Fertile Crescent region. Students can use a map scale to calculate the length of the land bridge and then consider how long it might have taken people to travel across it on foot from Siberia to North America. Students can use a map of the Fertile Crescent to talk about what is happening in the region today and the implications of war and unrest for archaeological research.

TIMELINE

More than 12,000 years ago	People first enter Americas
12,500 years ago	People settle at Monte Verde, Chile
11,000 years ago	People of Clovis culture hunt and gather in North America
10,400–7,800 years ago	First farmers at Abu Hureyra, Syria, and at other places in Fertile Crescent
10,000 years ago	End of last ice age; megafauna become extinct
9,300–8,100 years ago	People live at Çatalhöyük, Turkey
8,500 years ago	People live seasonally at Koster, Illinois
8,400 years ago	Kennewick Man dies in what is now United States
7,600 years ago	Mediterranean Sea floods Lake Euxine, creating Black Sea; people live year round at Koster, Illinois

UNIT PROJECTS

Getting Here

Divide volunteers into two groups, representing either the Monte Verde or Clovis people. Each group should research the following: when the people first came to the Americas, how they may have entered North America, and where and how they lived. Have each group share information orally with the class and use a map to show how they entered North America—either via the Bering Land Bridge or via a Pacific coastal route. The class as a whole can discuss the question "Was there more than one route by which people first entered the Americas?"

Dogs, Wolves, and Humans

Invite a small group of students to work on a group presentation about the evolution of wolves to dogs and the earliest relationship between dogs and humans. Students can use information from the chapters and from other sources, such as the article "From Wolf to Woof" by Karen E. Lange in the January 2002 issue of *National Geographic*.

A Long Time(line)

Many different events covering thousands of years are included in this unit. Students can make a long horizontal timeline for the classroom and include all the events, using different colors for events on different continents.

Farming vs. Hunting–Gathering

Assign two groups of students to create campaigns (posters, other visuals, speeches, and texts) to promote either farming or hunting-and-gathering to people of the Fertile Crescent 10,400 years ago. Make sure there are enough activities and features to involve all students in this research project. The Farmer–Domesticator group will campaign for a settled lifestyle and domestication of plants and animals. The Hunter–Gatherer group will promote the advantages of a varied diet and mobile lifestyle. The class can vote on which campaign is more persuasive.

Displaying Çatalhöyük

Students can create an annotated Çatalhöyük display based on information in Chapter 20 and on the Internet at *http://catal.arch.cam.ac.uk/visit/visitEN.html*. This site contains a visitor's guide, site map, and information about the excavations. Another site contains diary entries of people working at the Çatalhöyük dig: *http://ltc.smm.org/catal/updates*. In their display, students should explain what archaeologists have found and are hoping to find and why Çatalhöyük is important.

ADDITIONAL ASSESSMENT

For Unit 5, divide the class into groups and have them all undertake the Farming vs. Hunting–Gathering project so you can assess their understanding of the transition from a nomadic foraging and hunting lifestyle to a settled farming lifestyle. Use the scoring rubric at the back of this guide to assess students' work, and have students rate their own work with the self-assessment rubric.

LITERATURE CONNECTION

The following book will broaden students' knowledge of the settlement of North America.

▶ Lauber, Patricia. *Who Came First? New Clues to Prehistoric Americans.* Washington, DC: National Geographic, 2003. Nonfiction. This book explores the different theories about when humans first migrated to North and South America. Using maps, timelines, and artifacts, it also shows how science works to challenge old theories and propose new ones. AVERAGE

UNIVERSAL ACCESS

The following strategies are designed to cover a range of learning styles and reading, language, and skill levels.

Reading Strategies

▶ To facilitate reading, help students preview the artwork and captions in each chapter to make predictions about the content.

▶ Have students use a K-W-L chart (see the reproducible at the back of this guide) to assist them in their reading. Preview each chapter, and have students fill in the first column of the chart with what they *know* about the subject. Have them write what they *want to know* about the subject in the second column. When they are finished with the chapter, have them complete the third column by writing what they *learned*.

▶ Have students note the numerous sidebars in Unit 5 that describe events in prehistory. Students can add these events and dates to the class's Long Time(line) (see Unit Projects).

Writing Strategies

▶ Each chapter describes places where important evidence about human settlement has been found. Have students write brief descriptions of each place and give its significance.

▶ Have students summarize the archaeological evidence uncovered at one of the sites discussed in this unit. Ask them to summarize archaeologists' conclusions about the evidence and then draw their own conclusions.

▶ Have partners make a four-column chart with headings for each of the unit's big ideas—*Movement, Settlement, Diversity,* and *Change.* Partners should get together after reading each chapter to jot down their observations in the relevant categories.

Listening and Speaking Strategies

▶ To spark student involvement in the material, read the opening paragraph or two of each chapter and have students state their expectations for the chapter.

▶ As you read sections of each chapter aloud, ask volunteers to describe how they imagine different scenes. For example, students may describe a scene of people walking through the mile-wide pathway between two glaciers, or a large animal struggling in a tar pit. Volunteers can then develop the description into a scene they act out for the class.

UNIT VOCABULARY LIST

The following words that appear in Unit 5 are important for your students' understanding of the social studies content as well as for development of literacy. Use these words for vocabulary study or to reinforce language arts skills (e.g., synonyms, compound words, prefixes and suffixes, and related words). Words are listed in the order in which they appear in the chapters.

Chapter 17	Chapter 18	Chapter 19	Chapter 20
desperate	shock	domesticate	elaborately
mastodon	dehydration	parasite	sieves
formidable	frigid	nutrient	profession
obstacle	mammoth	malnutrition	specialization
glacier	forecast	agriculture	concentration
corridor	balmy	herbivore	
immigrant	hypothesis	carnivore	
migration	orphaned		
genetic	fertile		
heritage	flourishing		
riled	habitation		
discredit	paleoclimatologists		
edible	horizon		
medicinal	accumulation		

DOUBTING THOMAS: PEOPLING OF THE AMERICAS

PAGES 105–111

CAST OF CHARACTERS

Thomas Dillehay (DILL-uh-hay) professor of anthropology at the University of Kentucky; excavated Monte Verde, Chile, where he found artifacts 12,500 years old

Clovis People hunter–gatherers who lived in North America 11,200 to 10,900 years ago; developed distinctive spear points

Kennewick (KEN-uh-wick) **Man** 8,000 years ago; skeleton of a modern human found in 1996 in the state of Washington

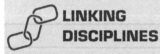

LINKING DISCIPLINES

Health Have students do additional research on medicinal plants like those found at Monte Verde. Have them compare medicinal plants to conventional medicines.

CHAPTER SUMMARY

The discovery that humans lived at Monte Verde, Chile, 12,500 years ago upset the conventional wisdom that the first humans to reach North America were a group of big-game hunters known as the Clovis people (named after the site where their artifacts were discovered). Archaeologists had to reconsider their long-held beliefs in light of the evidence at Monte Verde.

PERFORMANCE OBJECTIVES

▶ To understand the importance of the discovery at Monte Verde and what it meant to archaeologists
▶ To describe the Bering Land Bridge and why it was not a feasible route at the time people came to Monte Verde
▶ To appreciate the Clovis people, who, prior to the discovery at Monte Verde, were considered the first Americans

BUILDING BACKGROUND

Ask students to describe an experience where they knew they were wrong but refused to admit it. Have them relate that denial of the evidence to the reaction of some scientists to the evidence found at Monte Verde.

WORKING WITH PRIMARY SOURCES

Read aloud the quote from Thomas Dillehay's book, *The Settlement of the Americas*, from "first immigrants" (page 108) through "more diverse than we thought" (page 109). Discuss how the idea of diversity was received by scientists who believed the first Americans were the Clovis people.

GEOGRAPHY CONNECTION

Movement Distribute the blackline master for Chapter 17 and have students analyze the routes of human migration into and through the Americas.

READING COMPREHENSION QUESTIONS

1. What artifacts and other evidence did Thomas Dillehay find at Monte Verde? (*mastodon bones; wooden, bone, and stone tools; scraps of hides and meat; human footprints; hearths; edible and medicinal plants; wooden hut foundations*)

2. How did the Clovis people hunt mammoths? (*They developed razor-sharp spear points that caused mammoths to bleed to death.*)

3. What did most scientists believe about the first humans in the Americas before the Monte Verde findings? (*Most scientists believed that humans migrated over the Bering Land Bridge from Siberia to Alaska about 11,000 years ago, and then spread out across the Americas.*)

4. Why did some scientists try to discount Dillehay's findings at Monte Verde? (*The findings contradicted long-held beliefs about the first humans in the Americas.*)

CRITICAL THINKING QUESTIONS

1. How can you tell that the people living at Monte Verde had a complex social life? (*The people had different roles. They lived together in a long tent, with individual rooms, and came together for certain activities. They seemed to know about medicinal plants and either traveled to get them or traded for them. They lived in one place year-round and so were not always traveling to follow their food sources.*)

2. Summarize the present beliefs about how humans came to the Americas. (*Humans came to the Americas from Asia by different routes—coastal and inland—as well as at different times.*)

SOCIAL SCIENCES

Science, Technology, and Society   Have students learn more about the Clovis people and the Clovis points that they used for hunting and other work. One useful website is *www.crystalinks.com/clovis.html.*

READING AND LANGUAGE ARTS

Reading Nonfiction   This chapter's sidebars contain important information. Ask students to assess the sidebars' content and explain what each sidebar adds to their understanding of human migration in the Americas.

Using Language   Clarify the differences between mastodons and mammoths (and the relation of both to modern elephants) by having students locate a picture of a mammoth and a modern elephant to compare to the mastodon shown on page 105. Then ask them to describe the three animals in their own words.

SUPPORTING LEARNING

Struggling Readers   Have students place all the people mentioned in this chapter (Meadowcroft Rockshelter, Monte Verde, Clovis, Kennewick Man) along a timeline, with notes about what is known about each.

EXTENDING LEARNING

Enrichment   Students can investigate Meadowcroft Rockshelter, a site that may turn out to be older than Monte Verde. They can organize their findings, draw conclusions, and create a presentation to give to the class. Two online sources are *www.meadowcroftmuseum.org/rockshelter.htm* and *www.mnsu.edu/emuseum/archaeology/sites/northamerica/meadowcroft.html.*

Extension   Have students read the description of the specialized roles of people living at Monte Verde on page 111 and then sketch a scene showing families performing the different jobs mentioned.

WRITING

Compare/Contrast Encourage students to write a short essay comparing and contrasting the idea that one group entered the Americas "first" from one direction only with the idea that many groups entered the Americas at different times and from different directions.

THEN and **NOW**

In 2001 Thomas Dillehay stated, "Too much important archeology is played out through the press. This is very advantageous in many ways but dangerous in others." Ask students how they think reaction to the Monte Verde discovery might have influenced his opinion. Ask: Why might press coverage be advantageous to archaeology? Why might press coverage be dangerous?

COMING TO THE AMERICAS

Directions

Use the map and information from the chapter and other research to answer the questions. Write complete sentences.

1. What caused Beringia to exist? When did it exist?

_____

_____

_____

2. What stopped migration from Siberia to North America between 20,000 and 14,000 years ago?

_____

_____

_____

3. Use the map to determine the distance along the coastal route from Siberia to Monte Verde. Do the same for the inland route.

_____

_____

_____

4. Which do you think would have taken a shorter time—the coastal route from Siberia to Monte Verde or the inland route? Why?

_____

_____

_____

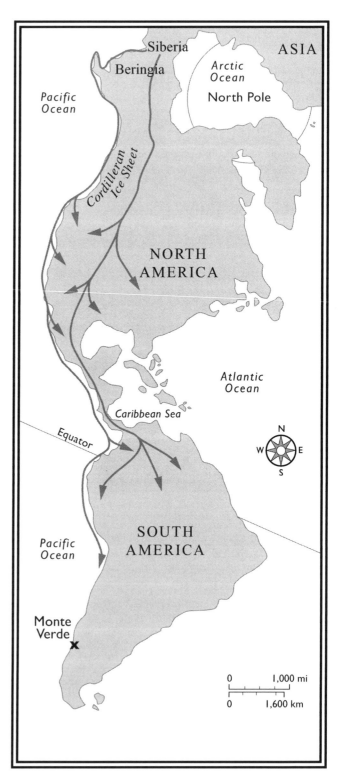

NAME   DATE

A. MULTIPLE CHOICE

Circle the letter of the best answer to each question.

1. Which of the following is **not** a reason many scientists at first rejected Monte Verde?
   a. They thought Dillehay had misinterpreted the evidence at the site.
   b. They wanted to continue believing that the Clovis people were the first Americans.
   c. They believed humans reached the Americas only via the Bering Land Bridge.
   d. They thought Dillehay was too young to make important discoveries.

2. The people who lived at Monte Verde could not have used the Bering Land Bridge during the period they came to the Americas because the Land Bridge was
   a. blocked by glaciers.   **c.** too far from Monte Verde.
   b. covered by seawater.   **d.** too muddy to walk across.

3. Thomas Dillehay believed he had discovered a prehistoric hospital when he found
   a. stone surgical instruments.   **c.** obsidian scalpels.
   b. medicinal plants.   **d.** wooden tongue depressors.

4. The Monte Verde people used cement made out of
   a. honey and gravel.   **c.** water, sand, and gravel.
   b. animal fat and sand.   **d.** animal fat and seaweed.

5. The evidence at Monte Verde shows that humans came to the Americas
   a. over the Bering Land Bridge.   **c.** to hunt mammoths.
   b. by different routes.   **d.** during the same time period.

B. SHORT ANSWER

Write one or two sentences to answer each question.

6. What theory about the origins of humans in the Americas did the Monte Verde discovery contradict?

_____

_____

7. How did the Clovis people get their food?

_____

_____

8. What other discoveries are changing the way archaeologists think about early humans in the Americas?

_____

_____

C. ESSAY

Write an essay on a separate sheet of paper giving your opinion of the following statement: The first people in the Americas were more diverse than we once thought. Support your opinion with details from the chapter.

THEN and **NOW**

Even after 44,000 years the La Brea Tar Pits are still dangerous to wildlife. In 2003 a flock of about 60 small birds landed and got stuck in an asphalt seep at Hancock Park, site of the tar pits.

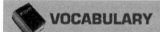 **VOCABULARY**

tundra vast, nearly level, treeless regions near the Arctic in Europe, Asia, and North America; has arctic climate and vegetation

CHAPTER SUMMARY

Two archaeological sites in the United States provide intriguing insights into Ice Age animals (La Brea Tar Pits in California) and over about 8,000 years of post–Ice Age social organization (Koster, Illinois).

PERFORMANCE OBJECTIVES

▶ To identify and describe the types of animals preserved in the La Brea Tar Pits
▶ To explain the significance of the mass extinction of giant mammals after the last ice age
▶ To understand what the horizons excavated at Koster have revealed to scientists about the lives of inhabitants 8,500 years ago

BUILDING BACKGROUND

Ask students what a typical family photo album includes and what they think future historians could learn about life today based on snapshots of us. Elicit ideas about what the chapter title means.

WORKING WITH PRIMARY SOURCES

Have students make a chart comparing the merits of the La Brea Tar Pits and Koster as "photo albums" of the prehistoric North American past. They can refer to the text and to primary source material in the chapter as evidence for their comparisons.

GEOGRAPHY CONNECTION

Interaction   Have students make a cause and effect chart to show what happened when the climate began warming after the last ice age. Have them list effects on plants, animals, and humans.

READING COMPREHENSION QUESTIONS

1. What did scientists find when they dug down into the La Brea Tar Pits? (*evidence of Ice Age animals and plants*)

2. What was found when scientists dug down into the earth at Koster, Illinois? (*evidence of 8,500 years of human habitation*)

3. What is distinctive about Horizons 11 and 10 at Koster? (*Horizon 11 contains the oldest cemetery in North America; Horizon 10 indicates that people worked at Koster but did not live there at that time.*)

4. What possessions were buried with people in Horizon 6? (*bone hairpins*)

CRITICAL THINKING QUESTIONS

1. What types of bones would you expect to find buried with mastodon bones at the La Brea Tar Pits? (*bones of predators that came to attack the trapped mastodon and were also trapped in the tar*)

2. What caused the people at Koster to stay there? (*After the Ice Age ended, people no longer had big game to hunt; they settled down and ate what they found locally.*)

3. Contrast the Overkill Hypothesis and the Climate Change Hypothesis for the extinction of the Ice Age megafauna. (*Overkill: humans killed off the giant Ice Age mammals; Climate Change: giant mammals died out in warmer weather when grasslands were replaced by trees.*)

SOCIAL SCIENCES

Science, Technology, and Society   Invite students to consider the hairpins illustrated on page 118 as evidence of the lifestyle of people in Horizon 6. Ask: What did settled lifestyle mean to the people in Horizon 6? Does a society with "stuff" always end up wanting more?

READING AND LANGUAGE ARTS

Reading Nonfiction   Point out the chapter title and have students identify the subjects of the two "photo albums." (*La Brea Tar Pits* and *Koster, Illinois*) Have students compare and contrast the way the authors present these two "albums." How much text is devoted to each? What illustrations and sidebars support the text in each section?

Using Language   Have students explain the play on words of the title of the It's the Pits sidebar on page 114.

SUPPORTING LEARNING

English Language Learners   Ask students to explain in their own words what is happening in the picture on page 113. Have them extend the scene to include the entrapment of predators attracted by the struggling mastodon. Then ask: How do we know this scene occurred?

Struggling Readers   Have students create a timeline of habitation at Koster. Students should label the timeline with the various levels of settlement and include details about each level.

EXTENDING LEARNING

Enrichment   Have students find out more about the discoveries made at the La Brea Tar Pits by visiting the Natural History Museum of Los Angeles County's website: *http://www.tarpits.org/education/guide/flora.*

Extension   Have volunteers act out different scenarios showing the first positive human–wolf interactions.

WRITING

Letter Invite students to write a letter describing their first day on the job as an excavator at the La Brea Tar Pits. They should base their letter on information in the sidebar on page 114. For a sense of on-the-job excitement, have them look at the picture on page 112.

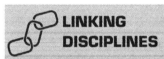

LINKING DISCIPLINES

Science Encourage students to find out more about how the La Brea Tar Pits were formed. They can find information from the Natural History Museum of Los Angeles County website: *http://www.tarpits.org/education/guide/flora.*

UNCOVERING KOSTER

Directions

Answer the questions based on the diagram of the excavations at Koster, Illinois.

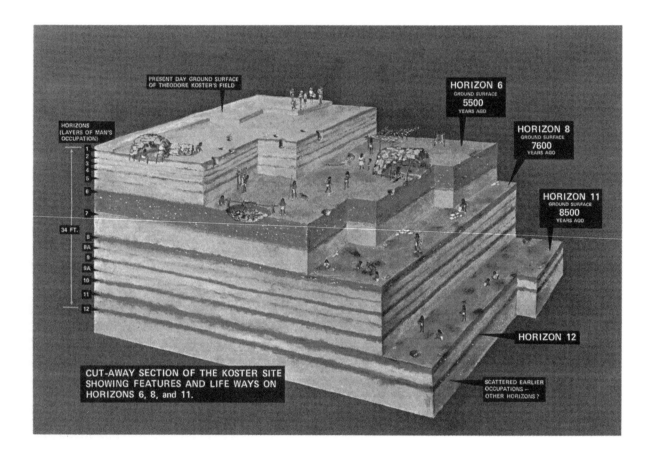

1. How many feet deep is the excavation at Koster?

_____

2. If you could go back to one of the horizons, which would you choose? What would you ask the people living there?

_____

_____

3. What is found on the top layer of Koster today? What do you predict the top layer will be a thousand years from now?

_____

_____

NAME   **DATE**

A. MULTIPLE CHOICE

Circle the letter of the best answer to each question.

1. How does the statement "There are 26 pancakes in the stack" relate to Koster, Illinois?
   a. There are 26 levels of human habitation at Koster.
   b. Archaeologists at Koster enjoyed hearty breakfasts.
   c. Artifacts at one level of Koster are piled 26 feet high.
   d. There are 26 theories about what happened to the people at Koster.

2. Why are the animal and plant remains in the La Brea Tar Pits so well preserved?
   a. Archaeologists took care of them.
   b. Oil formed a seal around them.
   c. They were not very old.
   d. Peat protected them.

3. Wolves and humans may have become friends because
   a. wolves liked cooked meat and humans needed protection.
   b. wolves and humans both needed protection from predators.
   c. wolves liked chasing humans and humans liked being chased.
   d. wolves needed help getting out of tar pits and humans liked feeling useful.

4. Which statement is true for both Koster and the La Brea Tar Pits?
   a. Megafauna skeletons were found there.
   b. Many human skeletons were found there.
   c. Excavations there have revealed evidence going back thousands of years.
   d. Excavations there have shown how people lived thousands of years ago.

5. What happened to the humans in the Americas when the large mammals died out?
   a. They migrated to other continents.
   b. They turned to farming.
   c. They had to change their entire lifestyle.
   d. They died out, too.

B. SHORT ANSWER

Write one or two sentences to answer each question.

6. What might have caused the mammoths to die out in the Americas?

   _____

   _____

7. Why did lions and sabretooth cats die out, too?

   _____

   _____

8. What animal was the first "pet" of the first Americans? How can you tell?

   _____

   _____

C. ESSAY

On a separate sheet of paper, write an essay explaining why you think so many different peoples used the Koster site over thousands of years.

STUDENT STUDY GUIDE

pages 47–48

THEN and NOW

In 2001, researchers from the University College London reported that new evidence from Abu Hureyra suggests that rye was cultivated there 13,000 years ago. If this is confirmed, it means that rye was the first cereal grain to be domesticated. Have students find food products that use rye.

 VOCABULARY

tell an Arabic word for a mound left by humans who lived in a given place

paleopathologists scientists who solve puzzles from the past and learn about ancient life from studying the dead

CHAPTER SUMMARY

Starting about 10,000 years ago, the world's first farmers left clues to their achievement at Abu Hureyra in Syria. The chapter focuses on scientists' detective work at Abu Hureyra and emphasizes the significance of the discoveries made there about the world's first farmers.

PERFORMANCE OBJECTIVES

▶ To understand how archaeologists used clues found in the skeletal remains of people at Abu Hureyra to determine how they lived
▶ To appreciate why the domestication of plants and animals was important to humans
▶ To identify some of the consequences of settlement and farming

BUILDING BACKGROUND

Start by asking students to describe the game "Twenty Questions." Point out that the answers to the 20 questions are clues that Player B uses to solve the mystery. Explain that in this chapter students will meet scientists who figured out clues given to them by bones.

WORKING WITH PRIMARY SOURCES

Based on information in the text, have students write captions for the four images of bones in this chapter. Then ask: Would these images be more meaningful if normal bones had been displayed with them for comparison?

GEOGRAPHY CONNECTION

Regions   Have students look at the map on page 122. Ask: What sources of fresh water run through the Fertile Crescent? (*Tigris River, Euphrates River, Nile River*) Which of these is closest to Abu Hureyra? (*Euphrates River*) What impact do these rivers have on the region? (*They supply a steady source of water and irrigation for cultivating crops.*)

READING COMPREHENSION QUESTIONS

1. Why was the site at Abu Hureyra so important to archaeologists? (*Since the site was occupied by hunter–gatherers and then farmers, they hoped to find the answer to why people changed from one lifestyle to the other.*)
2. How do we know that women at Abu Hureyra were the ones who ground flour? (*The toe bones of women were worn from hours of kneeling to grind flour with their toes curled under.*)
3. Why did scientists conclude that weavers and string makers lived in one area of Abu Hureyra? (*Skeletons with grooved teeth and large jaw bones—from holding cane in their teeth and chewing plants to make string—were found in only one area of the town.*)
4. What animals did the hunter–gatherers of Abu Hureyra eat? (*wild gazelles*) What animals did the farmers of Abu Hureyra eat? (*sheep, goats, pigs, cattle*)

CRITICAL THINKING QUESTIONS

1. Why is the work of paleopathologists like the work of detectives? (*Paleopathologists take the smallest clue—such as grooved teeth—and draw conclusions about ancient people based on the clue and what they know about ancient humans.*)

2. Summarize the possible reasons why people started to farm and domesticate animals. (*When people started to live in one place, their numbers increased. Farming feeds more people than hunting–gathering can. After the villagers had hunted all the gazelles, they domesticated and began to raise herd animals for meat.*)

3. What does the statement "What nature once directed, humans now controlled" mean? (*The plants and animals that once were wild had been domesticated by the first farmers.*)

SOCIAL SCIENCES

Economics   Have students use an almanac to get statistics on the decline in the number of farmers and farms in the United States. Have them relate this information to the idea that advancements in farming mean that fewer people can grow more food for a larger population. Have them compare farming in the United States today to agriculture in ancient societies such as Abu Hureyra. They should create charts and graphs to illustrate their comparison. Consider each stage of farming, and the labor, involved: What tasks once performed by many people can now be done by machinery?

READING AND LANGUAGE ARTS

Reading Nonfiction   Have students look at page 123 and identify the questions the authors pose. Have students determine whether the questions are answered in the text and how the questions help readers understand the topic.

Using Language   Help students pick out figurative expressions in the chapter, such as *race against the clock* (page 119) and *dig up enough clues* (page 120). Have students explain the meanings of these expressions.

SUPPORTING LEARNING

English Language Learners   Have students work with partners to define the words *reason/reasoning* and *deduce/deduction*. Then ask students to use the words in sentences and add them to the class word file.

Struggling Readers   Distribute copies of the blackline master for Chapter 19 and have students do the detective work with the information from Abu Hureyra.

EXTENDING LEARNING

Enrichment   Students can use Internet sources to learn more about what is being done to protect ancient sites in the Fertile Crescent.

Extension   Invite students to illustrate in cartoon style one of the Tips for Taming on page 124.

WRITING

Persuasion Ask students to write an essay to convince others that either farming or hunting-gathering is a desirable lifestyle.

Tell them to use information provided in the chapter to make their argument. Inform students that they will need to state their opinion clearly, provide evidence, and explain how their evidence supports their opinion.

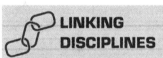

LINKING DISCIPLINES

Health Encourage students to learn more about protecting their bones and teeth. Though they don't face the same dangers and hardships faced by people in ancient Abu Hureyra, students need to know how to keep their bones and teeth healthy.

STORIES TOLD BY BONES AND TEETH

Directions

For each of the reasoning examples, fill in the clue that paleopathologists started with and the deduction they made about life in Abu Hureyra.

Clue Found at Abu Hureyra	Reasoning of Paleopathologists	Deduction Made by Paleopathologists
	Bones get bigger to support bigger muscles.	
	People catch and spread parasites when they are crowded together.	
	Skeletons with grooved teeth were found in only one area.	
	These big bones keep the head from wobbling.	
	Long hours of kneeling with toes curled under can cause these toe deformities.	

NAME   **DATE**

A. MULTIPLE CHOICE

Circle the letter of the best answer for each question.

1. Paleopathologists solve puzzles about the past by studying
  a. history books.
  b. people who died in ancient times.
  c. people today.
  d. living plants and animals.

2. Which phrase best describes the Fertile Crescent?
  a. region where farming began
  b. bread baked at Abu Hureyra
  c. tool used to harvest grain
  d. region where first hunter–gatherers lived

3. The villagers of Abu Hureyra threw their trash
  a. into community trash heaps.
  b. into the fire.
  c. out into the street.
  d. in the river.

4. All of the following are true about early farmers **except**
  a. they worked harder than hunter–gatherers.
  b. they lived near their animals.
  c. they had a more varied diet than hunter–gatherers.
  d. they could feed more people than hunter–gatherers.

5. The population of farming groups increased more than that of hunting groups because
  a. people living close together were less likely to get sick.
  b. farmers were less likely to be killed while hunting.
  c. people who stayed in one place could raise more children.
  d. people were better farmers than hunters.

B. SHORT ANSWER

Write one or two sentences to answer each question.

6. Why were archaeologists particularly interested in the tell at Abu Hureyra?

7. What are two of the deductions about the people of Abu Hureyra made by paleopathologists?

8. What things did the first farmers have to domesticate, or tame?

C. ESSAY

On a separate sheet of paper, write an essay comparing and contrasting the lifestyles of farmers and hunter-gatherers.

DEAR DIARY: ORIGINS OF SETTLED LIFE

PAGES 125–130

CAST OF CHARACTERS

James Mellaart British archaeologist who discovered Çatalhöyük

Ian Hodder British archaeologist who directs the excavations at Çatalhöyük

THEN and NOW

A great deal of information about the Çatalhöyük excavation is available online. An annual newsletter is posted in December each year. During periods of excavation people working at the site make their diary entries available on-line. The main Çatalhöyük website at *http://catal. arch.cam.ac.uk/index. html* has links to the above topics as well as to images and maps.

CHAPTER SUMMARY

Ten thousand people lived in Çatalhöyük nine thousand years ago, but does that mean it was a city? The chapter introduces the amazing archaeological finds that have been made at Çatalhöyük and raises the question "What did people do there?" Until that question is answered, Çatalhöyük will continue to be considered an overgrown village by many.

PERFORMANCE OBJECTIVES

▶ To understand what is known and what remains a mystery about Çatalhöyük
▶ To understand the definition of a city and measure Çatalhöyük against it
▶ To describe some of the excavation techniques and analyses carried out at Çatalhöyük

BUILDING BACKGROUND

Read the chapter title and discuss with students what a diary is and why it is useful. Ask them why they think people would keep a daily record of events. Ask about students' experiences with keeping a diary and elicit why it is important for people excavating an archaeological site to keep a daily record.

WORKING WITH PRIMARY SOURCES

Among the exciting discoveries at Çatalhöyük are the layers and layers of wall murals. Distribute the blackline master for Chapter 20 and have students evaluate the two interpretations of the mural.

GEOGRAPHY CONNECTION

Interaction   Have students read the description of the mud bricks used to build homes in Çatalhöyük. Ask them to evaluate the building materials available to the residents of the village.

READING COMPREHENSION QUESTIONS

1. Since Çatalhöyük had no streets, how did the inhabitants move around town? (*They walked on the roofs of houses, entering them through doorways in the roofs.*)
2. What mysteries about Çatalhöyük are archaeologists trying to solve? (*Possible answers: What did the people do at Çatalhöyük? Why were people buried under the floors of houses? What do the murals mean?*)
3. What evidence is there at Çatalhöyük that there were no specialists such as brick makers? (*The mud bricks used to build the houses are all different; a specialized brick maker would have made bricks that looked similar.*)

CRITICAL THINKING QUESTIONS

1. How do you think a city is different from a village? Do you agree with those scientists who call Çatalhöyük a city, or with those who think it is an overgrown village? (*Answers will vary. Students should support their opinions with details from the chapter as well as personal knowledge.*)
2. How do Ian Hodder's methods of excavating Çatalhöyük differ from those of James Mellaart? (*Mellaart worked quickly to take things out of the site. Hodder goes more slowly, painstakingly sifting dirt so as not to miss anything.*)

SOCIAL SCIENCES

Civics   Chapter 19 discusses the fact that when people live together in groups, problems develop. Brainstorm health and other problems that may have developed in Çatalhöyük. Have students consider how modern people would deal with these problems.

READING AND LANGUAGE ARTS

Reading Nonfiction   Ask students to read the chapter title and predict what the chapter will be about. When they have finished reading, have them identify the sections that reflect the title. Then have them decide whether the text lives up to the promise of the title.

Using Language   Help students compare and contrast the description of Mellaart's work at Çatalhöyük (page 126–127) with Hodder's work (page 127–128). Note the words that show the earlier work was fast and sloppy, whereas the current work is slow and painstaking.

SUPPORTING LEARNING

English Language Learners   Help students distinguish between a city and a village (page 129, first paragraph). Make sure they understand why a city would not be inhabited by farmers.

Struggling Readers   Have students make a two-column chart about Çatalhöyük with the headings *What Is Known* and *What Is Unknown*. Have students use the two columns to organize the information about Çatalhöyük found in the chapter.

EXTENDING LEARNING

Enrichment   Students can read a diary entry written by a scientist working at Çatalhöyük at *http://ltc.smm.org/catal/updates/archives/000535.html*. Have students summarize the information in their own words or create an oral presentation that includes reading the diary entry to the class.

Extension   Have partners read passages of the text to each other, particularly the diary entries, so that they understand the details. Encourage partners to ask each other questions about the passages they read.

WRITING

Ask students to write a paragraph responding to the statement "A defining feature of a town or city is [that] farmers don't live in them" (page 129).

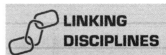

LINKING DISCIPLINES

Art Invite interested students to evaluate the "Mysteries" section of the Çatalhöyük's kids' website: *www.smm.org/catal/mysteries*. They can create a rubric to judge the comic-book format, overall design, ease of use, interest level of the mysteries, and other criteria of their choosing. Have them create an illustrated talk about the site, printing out some of the pages to illustrate their points.

NAME   DATE

WHAT IS IT? INTERPRETING ART FROM ÇATALHÖYÜK

Directions

Read the comments of two experts on Çatalhöyük who disagree about what this mural shows. Then answer the questions.

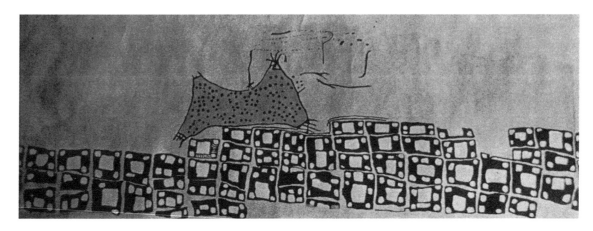

A. *It's a volcano.* James Mellaart, original excavator of Çatalhöyük in the 1960s, said:

"A clearer picture of a volcano in eruption could hardly have been painted: the fire coming out of the top, lava streams from vents at its base, clouds of smoke and glowing ash hanging over its peak . . . "

B. *It's a leopard skin.* Tristan Carter, a specialist working at Çatalhöyük today said:

" . . . [I]t looks quite a lot like the leopard skins that were painted elsewhere."

1. In these quotes neither scientist explains the squares that cover the bottom third of the mural. The caption in the text says some scientists think they are houses. How does that interpretation fit with the idea that the spotted shape is a leopard?

_____

_____

2. If the squares do not represent houses, what do you think they represent?

_____

3. What do you think the mural represents? You can choose one of the above interpretations and explain your choice. Or you can come up with your own interpretation. You can combine interpretations A or B with your own. Explain your choice on the lines below.

_____

_____

_____

_____

NAME   DATE

A. MULTIPLE CHOICE

Circle the letter of the best answer for each question.

1. Which of the following was **not** found at Çatalhöyük?
   a. built-in furniture   **c.** human skeletons
   b. paved streets   **d.** mud bricks

2. Which of the following describes Ian Hodder's approach to exploring Çatalhöyük?
   a. Use heavy equipment to immediately uncover as much of the site as possible.
   b. Immediately remove objects from the spot where they were found.
   c. Keep all explorations secret and reveal findings only to other scientists.
   d. Examine an object's relationship to its location before removing it.

3. Which statement describes the houses at Çatalhöyük?
   a. They were huts with thatched roofs and no furniture.
   b. They had bare walls that were never decorated.
   c. They were very large—the size of several school classrooms.
   d. They were new houses built over older ones.

4. Çatalhöyük is not considered a city by some scientists because they have found no evidence of
   a. specialized occupations.   **c.** many houses crowded together.
   b. a large number of people.   **d.** an interest in the arts.

5. Obsidian found at Çatalhöyük had been used for tools and
   a. floors.   **c.** mirrors.
   b. wall decoration.   **d.** ladders.

B. SHORT ANSWER

Write one or two sentences to answer each question.

6. What is one possible reason that the dead of Çatalhöyük were buried beneath their houses?

   _____

   _____

7. What did the residents of Çatalhöyük have to do to visit a neighbor?

   _____

   _____

8. What does the decoration of the inside of their houses show about the people of Çatalhöyük?

   _____

   _____

C. ESSAY

Use information from the chapter to write an essay on a separate sheet of paper describing the mysteries still being investigated at Çatalhöyük.

VOICES FROM THE PAST

PAGES 131–148

UNIT OBJECTIVES

Unit 6 covers the period from 5,300 to 1,200 years ago and takes readers from the Alps to Stonehenge, from the Sahara to Easter Island. In this unit, your students will learn

▶ how scientists interpreted clues revealed by human remains in Europe.
▶ how climate change in the Sahara affected agriculture.
▶ the results of Thor Heyerdahl's voyage to Polynesia.

PRIMARY SOURCES

Unit 6 includes pictures of the following artifacts:

▶ *Homo sapiens sapiens* remains, Ötzal Alps
▶ Bearskin cap, Ötzal Alps
▶ *Homo sapiens sapiens* remains, Amesbury, England
▶ Copper knives, Amesbury, England
▶ Stonehenge, Wiltshire, England
▶ Rock art, Wadi Teshuinat, Libya
▶ Ceramic vessel, Peru
▶ Stone house, Easter Island, Chile
▶ Stone fishhook, Easter Island, Chile
▶ Statues, Easter Island, Chile

BIG IDEAS IN UNIT 6

Evidence, movement, and **adaptation** are the big ideas in Unit 6. The bodies of Ötzi and the Amesbury Archer provide evidence of where they lived and what happened to them. The rock art of the Sahara is evidence of life before the climate there changed. The megaliths of Stonehenge and giant statues of Easter Island are evidence of mysteries still to be solved. People are on the move in these chapters, from an individual person on foot in the Alps to Thor Heyerdahl on a raft in the Pacific. Adaptation is seen in the Iceman's Bronze Age ax, the development of farming in the Sahara, and the ways people on Rapa Nui adapted to conditions in different parts of the island.

You can introduce these ideas by asking students to consider the connection between moving and adapting. Ask: Can you move through the world without adapting? What do you think of people who travel but refuse to adapt to the ways of the places they visit?

GEOGRAPHY CONNECTION

Refer students to the map on pages 12–13. You may want to provide more detailed maps of the Sahara and of Easter Island to help students visualize the relative size of these important places in the Unit. You could also refer students to a topographic map of the Ötzal Alps to give them an idea of the rugged mountains where the Iceman was found.

TIMELINE

5,300 years ago	Ötzi the Iceman is killed in Alps
5,000–3,500 years ago	Building and use of Stonehenge, England
4,500 years ago	Sahara Desert becomes dry; farming spreads south of Sahara
4,300 years ago	Beginning of Bronze Age in Europe; Amesbury Archer buried near Stonehenge
1,400–1,200 years ago	First peopling of Easter Island (Rapa Nui) and Hawaii

UNIT PROJECTS

Preserving Ötzi

Have a team of students investigate the methods by which remains like Ötzi's are preserved. Students can create a display showing the steps by which Ötzi was discovered, uncovered, transported, analyzed, and placed in a refrigerated display. Have the team poll classmates to find out their opinions about displaying Ötzi's remains.

Rock Art Today

Have a group of interested students report to the class about the rock art of the Sahara, including its current condition. They can find information and photographs at *www.libyarockart.com/geographic.htm*. The group can create an illustrated oral presentation that includes information about environmental threats to the rock art.

Giant Mysteries: Stonehenge and Rapa Nui

Invite two teams of students to use print or on-line resources to research efforts to solve the mysteries of how people moved giant stones at Stonehenge and Rapa Nui. For Rapa Nui they can check on-line at *www.pbs.org/wgbh/nova/easter*. For Stonehenge they can visit *http://exn.ca/mysticplaces/construction.asp*. Teams can create presentations summarizing their findings and giving their own theories about how the giant stones and statues were moved.

ADDITIONAL ASSESSMENT

For Unit 6, divide the class into groups and have them all undertake the Giant Mysteries: Stonehenge and Rapa Nui project so you can assess their understanding of the religious, social, and economic aspects of these monuments. Use the scoring rubric at the back of this guide to assess students' work, and have students rate their own work with the self-assessment rubric.

LITERATURE CONNECTION

There are numerous enjoyable books to broaden students' knowledge of archaeological discoveries around the world. For example,

► Heyerdahl, Thor. *Kon-Tiki: Across the Pacific by Raft.* New York: Buccaneer, 1999. The author gives his account of his voyage across the Pacific to explore his theory about how humans came to Polynesia. Nonfiction. ADVANCED

► Patent, Dorothy Hinshaw. *Secrets of the Ice Man* (Frozen in Time, Group 1). New York: Benchmark, 1998. Nonfiction. Forensic scientists and paleoanthropologists use the latest technology to examine the Ice Man who was discovered in the Alps in 1991. EASY

► Pelta, Kathy. *Rediscovering Easter Island: How History Is Invented.* New York: Lerner, 2001. Nonfiction. The book gives an overview of the history and exploration of Easter Island. AVERAGE

UNIVERSAL ACCESS

The following strategies are designed to cover a range of learning styles and reading, language, and skill levels.

Reading Strategies

► There are unfamiliar words in this unit that are not defined. Suggest that students add them to the class's word file. Students can create word cards for each chapter. On each card, students should write the word, define it, and use it in a sentence. They may illustrate the word, as well.

► Have partners read sections of the chapters to each other and then ask each other questions about the content: What is the main idea of this passage? What details or examples support the main idea?

► Have groups of three students read this unit, with each student taking one chapter. Each group member should take notes on the reading. Group members should come together to tell each other what they learned about the time and place covered by each chapter.

Writing Strategies

► Descriptions of scientists' work appear in each of the chapters in Unit 6. Have students create a two-column chart with the headings *Pure Investigation* and *Proving a Point*. Ask students to use the chart to record their conclusions (or best guess) about the scientists described in the chapter: Were they doing pure research? Were they trying to prove something that they already had strong opinions about?

► Have students work in small teams to write proposals requesting funds to erect a megalith monument in their town. Explain that for this part of the proposal, teams don't have to be concerned about the project's budget. Instead, they will describe the size of the megalith (height and weight), what it will commemorate, where it will go, and how it will be transported.

► There are strong visual images in each chapter in Unit 6. Have students choose one image from each chapter and write a script for a narrator talking about them on a television show called *Images of the Past*. The script should mention connections among the images—how they look, where they were found, how they were made, or simply how they inspire or puzzle the narrator.

Listening and Speaking Strategies

▶ Invite two small groups to create monologues—one for Ötzi and one for the Amesbury Archer. Each can speak about his travels, his health, his possessions, and why he was in the Ötzal Alps or England. Each group can create a monologue for a second speaker who comes in at the end to describe Ötzi's murder or the Amesbury Archer's burial. Groups can present their monologues to the class, either live or through a recording.

▶ Have a group of students hold a press conference in which they act as experts in Thor Heyerdahl's theories about the spread of Peruvian culture westward and answer questions posed by the rest of the class.

UNIT VOCABULARY LIST

The following words that appear in Unit 6 are important for your students' understanding of the social studies content as well as for development of literacy. Use these words for vocabulary study or to reinforce language arts skills (e.g., synonyms, compound words, prefixes and suffixes, and related words). Words are listed in the order in which they appear in each chapter.

Chapter 21	Chapter 22	Chapter 23
deteriorate	dune	trade wind
enamel	grazing	spore
colon		rigging
fertile		debris
arthritis		sacred
stroke		commission
intestines		
embers		
henge		

CAST OF CHARACTERS

Ötzi the Iceman (OOT-see) the well-preserved corpse of a man shot in the back with a bow and arrow

Amesbury Archer also called the king of Stonehenge; a wealthy man buried in southern England during the early Bronze Age

 VOCABULARY

megalith large stone used in prehistoric monuments

THEN and NOW

In 1998 Ötzi the Iceman was moved to a special cold storage chamber in the South Tyrol Museum of Archaeology, Bolsano, Italy. Museum visitors can view the Iceman through a small window.

CHAPTER SUMMARY

The analysis of the remains of two men who lived a thousand years apart reveals deep insights into their diets, deaths, travels, and possessions.

PERFORMANCE OBJECTIVES

▶ To identify and describe Ötzi and the Amesbury Archer and the evidence revealed through analysis of their remains
▶ To understand why Stonehenge is important and why the Archer may have some connection to it
▶ To appreciate the questions still to be answered about Ötzi and the Archer

BUILDING BACKGROUND

Ask students what they have heard or read about mummies (intentionally preserved human bodies) and/or the Iceman (who was preserved in ice for 5,300 years). Explain that this chapter has graphic information about what happens to a body when it dies and offers fascinating details about what analyzing a body can reveal to scientists.

WORKING WITH PRIMARY SOURCES

Invite students to look closely at the bearskin cap on page 133. Ask them to give their impressions of the hat and evaluate it as a primary source. What can a hat like this tell scientists about Ötzi and his life?

GEOGRAPHY CONNECTION

Place   Provide students with a detailed map of the Ötzal Alps, and ask students to observe what countries they are in and how high they are.

READING COMPREHENSION QUESTIONS

1. Where did Ötzi and the Amesbury Archer get their names? (*from the Ötzal Alps where Ötzi was found and the part of England where the Archer was found*)
2. How was Ötzi's body preserved for 5,300 years? (*His body was first covered with snow and then by a glacier. Since he was in a gully, he was not crushed by the ice.*)
3. Why did scientists conclude that the Archer of Amesbury was a rich man? (*from the number of valuable things buried with him*)
4. What is a henge, and why is Stonehenge called the "most famous" henge? (*A henge is an enclosure used for ceremonies. Stonehenge is famous for its massive megaliths and the mystery of how they were transported to the site.*)

CRITICAL THINKING QUESTIONS

1. Why did the copper ax found with Ötzi's body confuse scientists? (*Ötzi died during what is considered the Stone Age, so scientists wonder where he got a copper ax.*)
2. What did scientists discover about farming in Europe from Ötzi's body? (*They found evidence of bread made from wheat that was farmed, not wild.*)
3. Why is the evidence provided by the remains of Ötzi and the Archer important? (*It broadens our understanding of what the world was like 5,300 and 4,300 years ago, respectively.*)
4. What are some of the ways the Archer's life differed from Ötzi's? (*He had traveled farther; he had more possessions; and many of his possessions were metal.*)

SOCIAL SCIENCES

Science, Technology, and Society   Invite interested students to find out more about how forensic anthropologists drew conclusions about where Ötzi and the Archer lived and traveled from examining their tooth enamel.

READING AND LANGUAGE ARTS

Reading Nonfiction   In the first sentence of the chapter, the authors write "the Iceman has a lot to say." Ask students to identify evidence in the chapter that supports this statement and to decide if the evidence is adequate.

Using Language   Analyze the "Q and A" sessions the authors describe between scientists and Ötzi. Have students visualize the way that scientists asked the Iceman questions—by performing an autopsy—and how Ötzi answered.

SUPPORTING LEARNING

English Language Learners   To help students understand the details of where the Iceman was found and why his body was untouched for more than five thousand years, sketch the scene in the first paragraph on page 132. Label the gully and ridges mentioned in the text.

Struggling Readers   Distribute the blackline master for Chapter 21. Students can complete the chart to review the main discoveries that scientists have made about the Iceman and the Archer.

EXTENDING LEARNING

Enrichment   Students can use print resources and the website *www.stonepages.com/england/england.html* to learn more about the timeline of Stonehenge's construction and use. They can give a presentation to the class showing Stonehenge on a map and explaining the highlights of its history and present state.

Extension   Have students act out scenes from the Iceman's saga: his being discovered by hikers; his being mistakenly identified as a modern person; and subsequent revelations about him and efforts to preserve him.

 **WRITING**

Dialogue Have students imagine that they can speak with Ötzi and the Archer. Ask them to write a dialogue in which they pose questions, and Ötzi and the Archer answer them. (For some of the answers, students can use their imaginations.)

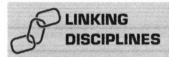 **LINKING DISCIPLINES**

Economics Invite students to consider the connection between farming and luxury items spelled out on page 135. Ask: How reliable would farming be as a source of trade goods? How much uncertainty would there be from season to season? Do people today see farming as the best way to get luxury items? What has changed?

NAME _____   DATE _____

COMPARING ÖTZI AND THE ARCHER OF AMESBURY

Directions

Use information from the chapter to complete the chart comparing and contrasting Ötzi and the Archer.

	Ötzi	Archer of Amesbury
Where was he found?		
How old was he when he died?		
Explain his alternate name.		
What possessions were found with him?		
What do we know about his diet?		
What do we know about his health?		
What do we know about his travels?		
What mystery has he still not revealed?		

NAME   DATE

A. MULTIPLE CHOICE

Circle the letter of the best answer for each question.

1. How was Ötzi killed?
   a. He fell into a crevasse.
   b. He was stranded on the mountain and died of exposure.
   c. He was shot in the back by an arrow.
   d. He was attacked by wolves.

2. Scientists think that the Archer may have been connected to Stonehenge because
   a. he was evidently rich and powerful.
   b. he was buried at Stonehenge.
   c. people in his time called him the king of Stonehenge.
   d. he was a well-traveled person.

3. Scientists can learn all the following from examining tooth enamel **except**
   a. what possessions the person had.   **c.** where the person grew up.
   b. where the person traveled.   **d.** where the person lived as an adult.

4. Which of the following statements describes both Ötzi and the Archer?
   a. They were about 40 years old and suffered physically while alive.
   b. They lived in England and had many metal tools and weapons.
   c. They were murdered in the Alps, possibly by robbers.
   d. They were buried in elaborate graves near Stonehenge.

5. Which of the following describes how early Stonehenge looked?
   a. circular bank and ditch   **c.** circle of small stones found on the site
   b. circle of megaliths from far away   **d.** flat land where people stood in a circle

B. SHORT ANSWER

Write one or two sentences to answer each question.

6. Why do the authors say "Ötzi understood physics"?

_____

_____

7. How did the Archer's Bronze Age burial differ from most Stone Age burials?

_____

_____

8. What possible explanation could there be for Stone Age Ötzi having a copper ax?

_____

_____

C. ESSAY

On a separate sheet of paper, write an essay explaining why *rich* is a word that can describe a Bronze Age person but not someone from the Stone Age. Use details about the Archer and Ötzi to support your main idea.

GOT MILK? FARMING IN AFRICA

PAGES 137–141

Graeme Barker English professor of archaeology who led a Sahara expedition in 2002

THEN and NOW

The Sahara climate may be getting colder in the 21st century. In 2000, three people froze to death in the desert area of Mauritania, a West African country where people were completely unprepared for temperatures in the low 20s F. The opposite problem—extreme heat—is more usual. Temperatures can reach 122°F in Mauritania in the summer.

CHAPTER SUMMARY

About 7,000 years ago the Sahara Desert was a grassland interspersed with lakes and marshes. Evidence of the lives of people who lived there, and the animals they hunted and domesticated, has been found in the rock paintings and carvings they left behind. With the coming of climate change in the Sahara about 4,500 years ago, traditional ways of gaining food had to change.

PERFORMANCE OBJECTIVES

▶ To explain why agricultural innovations usually move more easily east and west than north or south
▶ To understand the evidence of lifestyles revealed in rock art
▶ To describe how the climate in the Sahara today differs from that of 7,000 years ago

BUILDING BACKGROUND

Ask students to describe what they think of when they hear the word *desert*. Explain that some places that are deserts today were grassy and wet a few thousand years ago. Tell students that in this chapter they will be viewing the same place—the Sahara Desert—in two different ways.

WORKING WITH PRIMARY SOURCES

Have students examine the rock art on page 141. Then ask them to list the questions they have about this image: for example, how big is the rock art? Have students see how many questions they can answer after they have finished reading.

GEOGRAPHY CONNECTION

Movement   Distribute the blackline master for Chapter 22 and have students answer questions based on the map.

READING COMPREHENSION QUESTIONS

1. What were the scientists in the chapter looking for in the Sahara? (*evidence that would show how people there changed from foragers to farmers and whether farming came about from climate change*)
2. What evidence did scientists discover that convinced them that farmers in the Sahara had tamed Barbary sheep? (*They found stalls that had been built to hold sheep.*)
3. What did scientists discover about the domestication of animals in the Sahara? (*They learned that domestication started 7,000 years ago; it did not arrive with colonists 6,000 years ago.*)
4. What was the Sahara like 7,000 years ago compared to today? (*then: an area of grassland, lakes, and marshes; now: a waterless desert*)

CRITICAL THINKING QUESTIONS

1. What made farming relatively easy in the Fertile Crescent? (*mild wet winters, dry summers, wild plants with big seeds*)

2. How did climate affect the spread of farming north from the Fertile Crescent? (*Harsh winters in northern Europe made autumn planting impossible; forests in Europe made it difficult to herd animals.*)

3. Explain the statement "As long as farming moves east and west, crops, tools and methods don't have to change." (*Temperatures, hours of daylight, and amount of rainfall change less when moving east to west than when moving north to south.*)

4. How did climate shift in the Sahara lead to the domestication of plants? (*People moved south when the climate changed, but wild plants there did not yield enough to feed the population. Therefore, people began to cultivate plants.*)

SOCIAL SCIENCES

Science, Technology, and Society   Have students consider this statement: When agriculture moves east to west, people can use similar tools, but when it moves north, farmers need to invent different tools. Ask students to investigate examples of tools that northern farmers had to invent and report their findings to the class.

READING AND LANGUAGE ARTS

Reading Nonfiction   The chapter is organized around a field trip made by members of the Prehistoric Society. Have students determine the number of paragraphs devoted to the scientists' adventures and evaluate what their story adds to the chapter.

Using Language   Have students define the words *cereal* and *serial* and consider the different meanings of *cereal*, distinguishing between the way it is used in this chapter and the way it is used at breakfast.

SUPPORTING LEARNING

Struggling Readers   To review the chapter's main points, have students make an annotated timeline starting with the appearance of the first farmers in the Fertile Crescent, and including the domestication of animals in the Sahara, climate change in the Sahara, and the domestication of plants in the Sahara region.

EXTENDING LEARNING

Enrichment   Students can use Internet sources to learn more about the Sahara's change from grassland to desert 4,500 years ago and what its future climate may be. Have students create a poster to display their findings.

Extension   Have students list the subjects of the rock art mentioned in the chapter (and shown in the illustrations on pages 140 and 141). They can find more pictures of rock art online at *www.manntaylor.com/rockart.html*.

WRITING

Narrative Have students read the Weird Crops sidebar on page 141 and describe a meal made with the three items mentioned as well as other foods mentioned in the chapter.

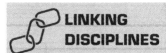

LINKING DISCIPLINES

Health Invite interested students to research the tsetse fly's impact on humans and animals in Africa today.

THE SPREAD OF FARMING

Directions

Study the map showing the spread of farming west from the Fertile Crescent. Then answer the questions.

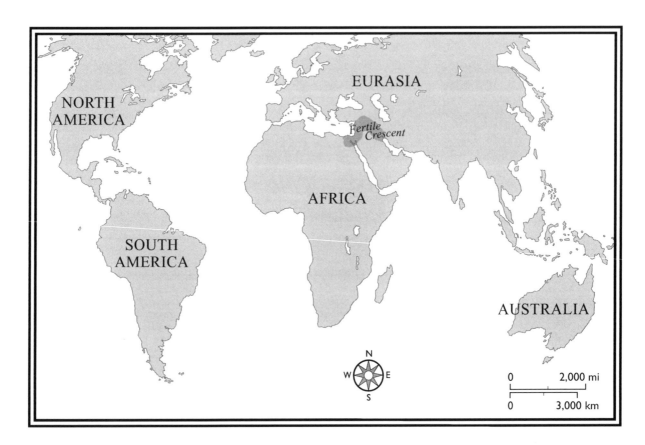

1. On the map, use arrows to show the directions in which agriculture first moved from the Fertile Crescent.

2. Shade the area that is now the Sahara Desert, and label it.

3. Draw arrows to show in which direction the farmers in the Sahara headed when the climate changed about 4,500 years ago.

4. On the lines, list which animals, as shown in the rock art, lived in the Sahara in the past. Put an **H** next to the animals that were hunted and a **D** next to the animals that were domesticated.

_____

_____

_____

_____

NAME   **DATE**

A. MULTIPLE CHOICE

Circle the letter of the best answer for each question.

1. Which of these statements does **not** describe farming in the Sahara?
   a. Farmers herded sheep.
   b. Farmers milked cows.
   c. Farmers grew yams and rice.
   d. Farmers grew sorghum and millet.

2. Which of the following blocked the spread of farming north from the Fertile Crescent?
   a. the tsetse fly
   b. wet summers
   c. harsh winters
   d. desert heat

3. Which of the following was **not** represented in Sahara rock paintings?
   a. elephant
   b. cow
   c. giraffe
   d. horse

4. People in the north of Europe were not farming and herding until many generations later than people in the Fertile Crescent because
   a. hunting was too good in the forests.
   b. they traded for food with the people in the Fertile Crescent.
   c. growing conditions were so different from those in the Fertile Crescent.
   d. they did not develop the tools necessary for that lifestyle.

5. Rock art in the Sahara shows all the following activities **except**
   a. herding sheep.
   b. milking cows.
   c. trapping ostriches.
   d. hunting mammoths.

B. SHORT ANSWER

Write one or two sentences to answer each question.

6. What evidence has been found that Saharan people herded sheep thousands of years ago?

7. How did the people of the Sahara get their food 7,000 years ago?

8. Why did increasing population make people turn to farming as a source of food?

C. ESSAY

The Sahara can be described in contradictory images depending on the period being discussed. On a separate sheet of paper, write an essay explaining how these varying conditions in the Sahara— hot, waterless, and sandy area; forested jungle with lots of rain; grassland with lakes and marshes—affected the people who herded and farmed there.

WESTWARD, NO! THE PEOPLING OF THE PACIFIC

PAGES 142-148

Thor Heyerdahl (tor HI-yer-dahl) Norwegian explorer and archaeologist who made long ocean voyages on simple boats and rafts

THEN and NOW

Plans have been made for a replica of Thor Heyerdahl's balsa raft *Kon-Tiki* to make a repeat voyage from Peru to Tahiti. This time scientists will be studying environmental threats to the oceans. One of Heyerdahl's grandsons is among the crew of the new raft, which will use solar panels to help transmit pictures to the Internet.

CHAPTER SUMMARY

Thor Heyerdahl made his historic trip on the raft *Kon-Tiki* from Peru to Polynesia to prove a hypothesis that he was convinced was true—that people had migrated west across the ocean from America to Polynesia thousands of years before. The truths about the islands he explored turned out to be far different than he expected.

PERFORMANCE OBJECTIVES

▶ To identify Thor Heyerdahl and describe his trips by sea to and around Polynesia

▶ To understand how archaeological evidence points to different conclusions than Heyerdahl predicted

▶ To describe the still-unanswered mysteries about the Easter Island statues

BUILDING BACKGROUND

Ask students to describe someone who is willing to risk everything, even his or her life, to prove something. Ask: In your experience, how would others react to such a person? Would they encourage the person? How would others react if the person succeeded? Explain that in this chapter they will meet a courageous scientist who faced positive and negative reactions to his quest for knowledge.

WORKING WITH PRIMARY SOURCES

Have students consider the three primary source images from Rapa Nui. Ask: What links these artifacts, besides their place of origin? (*All three are made of stone.*)

GEOGRAPHY CONNECTION

Location Distribute copies of the blackline master for Chapter 23 so that students can learn more about latitude and longitude.

READING COMPREHENSION QUESTIONS

1. What did experienced sailors tell Heyerdahl would happen to his raft? (*The logs would soak up seawater, and the raft would get heavy and sink.*)

2. What other dangers did Heyerdahl face on his long trip by raft? (*the possible breakup of his raft because of the ropes' disintegrating*)

3. Why did Heyerdahl make the trip from Polynesia to Rapa Nui? (*to show that Peruvians could have sailed to Rapa Nui*)

4. What other mystery did Heyerdahl try to solve on Rapa Nui? (*how the giant statues were moved from the quarry to their platforms*)

CRITICAL THINKING QUESTIONS

1. Summarize the criticisms made of Heyerdahl's theories even after he succeeded in reaching Polynesia on his raft. (*The Peruvians did not use sails, as he had; Peruvian rafts were smaller than the Kon-Tiki; and rafts were impractical for moving people and animals thousands of miles.*)

2. What evidence did Heyerdahl need to find on Rapa Nui to prove that people from Peru had settled the island? (*Heyerdahl needed to find artifacts that were similar to those used in Peru and different from those used in the rest of Polynesia; plants similar to those in Peru; and evidence of Peruvian techniques in making tools.*)

SOCIAL SCIENCES

Science, Technology, and Society   Have students find out more about the Rapa Nui statues and society. They can find information on the Internet at *www.sscnet.ucla.edu/ioa/eisp*.

READING AND LANGUAGE ARTS

Reading Nonfiction   Have students use the main idea map graphic organizer in the back of this guide to identify the assumptions on which Thor Heyerdahl based his theory that Peruvians first settled Polynesia. For each assumption, students should state how other scholars discredited it.

Using Language   Have students list words from the chapter having to do with the ocean: *swells, trade winds, spray, crew, cast off,* and so on. Ask them to define the words in their maritime context.

SUPPORTING LEARNING

English Language Learners   Have small groups of students read sections of the text together and take notes.

Struggling Readers   Have students refer to the map on page 145 as they explain the significance of Peru, Polynesia, and Rapa Nui in the chapter.

EXTENDING LEARNING

Enrichment   Students can use Internet sources to learn more about Thor Heyerdahl and to prepare biographical highlights to share with the class.

Extension   Have partners read aloud the chapter up to page 145, concentrating on the paragraphs that describe the experience of being on the *Kon-Tiki*. Partners should ask each other questions about the experience.

 **WRITING**

Persuasion Have students write a short essay in response to this comment (made to Heyerdahl by a fellow scientist): "The task of science is investigation pure and simple. Not to try and prove this or that." Students should state a clear position and support it with evidence, anticipating readers' responses.

 **LINKING DISCIPLINES**

Science Interested students can find out more about how scientists are using human DNA to track the movement of ancient people across the world.

LOCATING A SPOT ON THE EARTH

Directions

Read the information and the map, and then answer the questions.

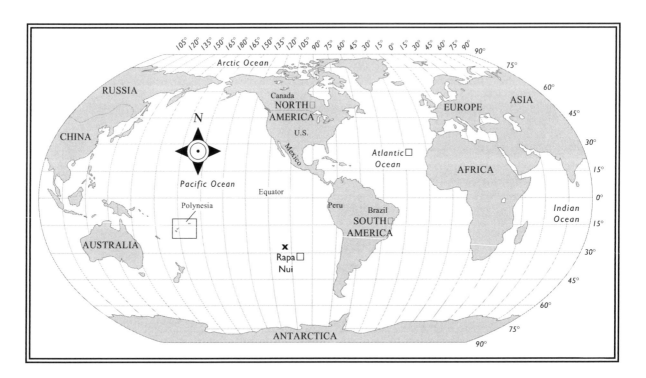

There are two ways to tell where something is located on the Earth. The first way is to give the **relative location** of the place. For example, you might tell a friend that you live seven blocks east of your school. Looking at the map, you might say that Rapa Nui is west of Peru. In both cases, you have located one place in relation to another place.

The second way is to give the **absolute location** of the place. You do this by stating the latitude and longitude of the place. Look at the map. The lines running horizontally across the map are lines of **latitude.** These measure distance north and south from the equator (which is marked 0°) to the North and South Poles (90°). The lines running vertically up and down the map are lines of **longitude.** These measure distance east and west from the prime meridian, which runs through Greenwich, England, and is marked 0°.

You can identify a location by stating its longitude and latitude. For example, Chicago, Illinois, is at 42°N latitude, 88°W longitude, or 42°N, 88°W. If you can't tell the exact latitude and longitude, you can say which lines the place is near.

1. Using the map, find the relative location of Polynesia. Write a complete sentence.

_____

2. Using the map, find the absolute location of Rapa Nui. Write a complete sentence.

_____

NAME   DATE

A. MULTIPLE CHOICE

Circle the letter of the best answer for each question.

1. Which of the following was **not** a reason that Thor Heyerdahl wanted to sail from Peru to Polynesia?
   a. to test his crew and himself against the sea for money
   b. to test a theory that other scientists thought was wrong
   c. to prove that Peruvians could have settled Polynesia
   d. to prove that a balsa wood raft would hold up in the Pacific Ocean

2. Heyerdahl's raft, *Kon-Tiki*, had room for
   a. Heyerdahl alone   **c.** Heyerdahl and five crew members
   b. Heyerdahl and one crew member   **d.** Heyerdahl, a crew, plants, and animals

3. Rapa Nui was named Easter Island because
   a. the island is shaped like an Easter egg.   **c.** *Rapa Nui* means "Easter."
   b. homes on the island all face east.   **d.** it was discovered on Easter Sunday.

4. People living in different parts of Rapa Nui had different occupations. Which of the following occupations is **not** one of them?
   a. cutting down trees   **c.** building rafts
   b. working with obsidian   **d.** growing bananas

5. Heyerdahl wanted to prove that the giant Easter Island statues
   a. were similar to South American statues.
   b. had walked by themselves from the quarry to their platforms.
   c. could be moved in an upright position.
   d. could be carried on people's shoulders.

B. SHORT ANSWER

Write one or two sentences to answer each question.

6. What did Heyerdahl believe proved that Polynesia was settled by people from Peru?

_____

_____

7. What evidence contradicted Heyerdahl's beliefs?

_____

_____

8. What effect did the construction of the giant heads on Rapa Nui eventually have on the residents of the island?

_____

_____

C. ESSAY

Write an essay on a separate sheet of paper summarizing the outcomes of Thor Heyerdahl's two trips described in the chapter.

COMPLEX SOCIETIES

PAGES 149–161

UNIT OBJECTIVES

Unit 7 covers the period from 4,000 years ago to 500 years ago. In this unit, your students will learn

▶ how agriculture in the Americas differed from agriculture in Europe.
▶ how the cultivation of wild corn resulted in the development of the familiar ears and kernels of corn today.
▶ what complex societies in North America were like between a thousand and five hundred years ago.

PRIMARY SOURCES

Unit 7 includes pictures of the following artifacts:

▶ Squash seed, Oaxaca, Mexico
▶ Paleofeces, Hinds Cave, Texas
▶ Building foundations, Cahokia, Illinois
▶ Monk's Mound, Cahokia, Illinois
▶ Storage pot, Cahokia, Illinois
▶ Serpent Mound, Peebles, Ohio
▶ Travois trails, Stanton, North Dakota
▶ Bison bones, Alberta, Canada
▶ Harpoon, Ozette, Washington

BIG IDEAS IN UNIT 7

Agriculture and **lifestyle** are the big ideas in Unit 7. Chapter 24 distinguishes the agriculture of the Americas from agriculture in Europe and discusses how agricultural practices influenced lifestyles in different parts of the world. Chapter 25 introduces the complex societies and varied lifestyles of North Americans before contact with Europeans. You may want to introduce this idea by eliciting from students what they know about the Americas before contact.

GEOGRAPHY CONNECTION

You can refer students to the map on pages 12–13 to locate the places mentioned in Unit 7. You may want to provide more detailed modern maps of North America and have students locate the sites mentioned in this chapter. Cahokia, for example, is near present-day St. Louis.

TIMELINE

10,000 years ago	Oldest evidence of farming in the Americas.
1,000 years ago	Native American peoples live in villages beside Knife River in North Dakota.
1,000–750 years ago	As many as 15,000 people live at Cahokia, Illinois.
930 years ago	Native Americans build Serpent Mound in Ohio.
500 years ago	Makah Indians occupy the village of Ozette, Washington.

UNIT PROJECTS

Corn: An Autobiography

Have a group of students create and perform "The Autobiography of Corn." Students can play different roles to depict corn's early years as the wild and spindly teosinte; its "discovery" and "taming" by people in Mesoamerica; its travels throughout the Americas and its increasing popularity there; and its current form, which has large plump kernels. Students can end with a "chorus line" of corn's roles today: corn syrup, cornmeal, cornstarch, popcorn, ethanol, and so on.

Taking Shelter in North America

Invite a group of students to locate more information about the housing used by each of the complex societies in Chapter 25. Have them create a presentation for the rest of the class that covers details such as materials used for building, construction techniques, number of people housed in each shelter, location of water and cooking fires, and information about chiefs' or priests' residences, if different.

Competing Crops

Have groups of students research the major types of grains grown around the world, such as corn, wheat, rye, oats, and sorghum. Students should find out the amounts of each grain harvested, the best growing conditions for each one, the distribution of each grain, how each grain is used, and the nutritional value of each grain, and the dollar value of the annual crop. Have groups create visual displays about their grains, including graphs. Groups can display their work in the class or present their information orally.

Different Settings, Different Societies

The complex societies discussed in Chapter 25 developed in widely separated settings that had extremely different environments. Have groups of students use the library/media center to investigate further the interaction between each group of people and their environment. Groups can use poster paper to make large cause-and-effect charts with pictures or drawings representing the ways in which each group used the resources that were available to them.

ADDITIONAL ASSESSMENT

For Unit 7, divide the class into groups and have them all undertake the Taking Shelter in North America project so you can assess their understanding of how the various groups of early Americans lived. Use the scoring rubric at the back of this guide to assess students' work, and have students rate their own work with the self-assessment rubric.

LITERATURE CONNECTION

▶ Aliki. *Corn Is Maize: The Gift of the Indians.* New York: HarperCollins Children's Books, 1996. Nonfiction. The book provides a description of how corn was discovered and used by the Indians and how it came to be an important food throughout the world. EASY

▶ Childress, Diana. *Prehistoric Peoples of North America.* New York: Chelsea House, 1996. Nonfiction. The book highlights the struggle to survive in North America in prehistoric times. EASY

▶ Shemie, Bonnie. *Mounds of Earth and Shell: Native Sites: The Southeast.* Plattsburgh, NY: Tundra Books of Northern New York, 1994. The book explores and describes the mysterious ancient mounds in the Southeast, which are evidence of a vast, complex civilization. EASY

UNIVERSAL ACCESS

The following strategies are designed to cover a range of learning styles and reading, language, and skill levels.

Reading Strategies

▶ Add definitions of unfamiliar words to the class's word file. Encourage students to review all the words in the file, and announce that you will be holding a reverse spelling bee. Deal out the word file cards to small groups of students. Call on each group in turn to be the "Challenger" and spell a word out loud, reading off the card. Students in other groups volunteer to be "Responders," defining each word and using it in a sentence. Award points for correct definitions and word uses.

▶ Call on students to play tour guide by reading sections of Chapter 25 aloud expressively. Fit the reading passages to each student's ability.

▶ Have partners read sections of the chapters to each other. The partners should alternate taking notes using the outline graphic organizer at the back of this guide. They can then review the main ideas of the chapters and their supporting details or examples.

Writing Strategies

▶ Have students further investigate some of the foods mentioned—chocolate, tomatoes, corn, chilies. Ask them to write a short essay comparing and contrasting the cultivation and use of one of these foods centuries ago with its cultivation and use today.

▶ Have students write a journal entry describing a visit to either Guilá Naquitz Cave (10,000 years ago) or Hinds Cave (2,000 years ago). Have them include a sample menu, describe activities around the cave, and note the time of year it was occupied.

▶ Have students use the cause and effect T-chart at the back of this guide to identify the relationship between farming techniques or environmental factors and lifestyle in Europe and the Americas.

▶ Have students make a four-column chart to use in comparing the sites toured in Chapter 25. In the first column, they should list the section headings (*Accomodations, Things to Do,* and so on). They should complete the chart with details from each site.

Listening and Speaking Strategies

► Point out the question on page 150: "Why didn't Native Americans 'discover' Spain?" Challenge a group of students to identify the follow-up questions and answers in the text and summarize the information orally for the class.

► Assign groups different sections of Chapter 25. Challenge them to do additional research beyond the chapter to become specialized tour guides for their assigned site. Tour guides can then make oral presentations to the class encouraging the audience to visit and explaining trip highlights.

UNIT VOCABULARY LIST

The following words that appear in Unit 7 are important for your students' understanding of the social studies content as well as for development of literacy. Use these words for vocabulary study or to reinforce language arts skills (e.g., synonyms, compound words, prefixes and suffixes, and related words). The words are listed below in the order in which they appear in the chapters.

Chapter 24
bungled
bizarre
leprosy
cacao
millstones
toil
artificial selection
paleofeces

Chapter 25
destination
accommodations
amenities
granary
extinguish
sweat lodge
travois
nominal
pemmican
barracks
accessorize
triathlon
tendon

MUTANT EARS TAKE OVER: THE ORIGINS OF FARMING IN THE AMERICAS   PAGES 149–153

THEN and NOW

In 2004 the National Museum of the American Indian opened on the National Mall in Washington, D.C. The ultimate goal of the museum is to help visitors "walk away with a sense of their own origins and the origins of the United States and all nations in the Western Hemisphere." In the museum, visitors will find the Mitsitam Café serving meals and snacks "based on the indigenous foods and culinary traditions of the Americas." *Mitsitam* is a Piscataway/Delaware word meaning "let's eat."

CHAPTER SUMMARY

Agriculture in the Americas was very different from agriculture in Europe. This chapter explores the extent to which agriculture dictates lifestyles and considers the question "Why didn't people of the Americas 'discover' Spain instead of the other way around?"

PERFORMANCE OBJECTIVES

▶ To explain how domestication of plants and animals unfolded in the Americas
▶ To understand the evolution of corn
▶ To identify the evidence revealed by an analysis of what people ate

BUILDING BACKGROUND

Ask students how they feel about trying new foods, such as dishes from cultures different from their own, exotic fruits, or new recipes made with familiar ingredients. Have adventurous and less adventurous eaters describe their likes and dislikes. Explain that in this chapter they will learn how foods travel from place to place and change the way people eat.

WORKING WITH PRIMARY SOURCES

Have students consider the paleofeces shown on page 153 and discuss the kind of evidence scientists have learned from it.

GEOGRAPHY CONNECTION

Location   Have students use the map on pages 12–13 or a larger map of North and South America to understand what is meant by "the Americas." On a detailed map they can locate places mentioned in the text such as the Andes Mountains, Mesoamerica (they will need guidance for this), Mexico, and Texas (the map on pages 12–13 shows the exact locations of caves mentioned in the text).

READING COMPREHENSION QUESTIONS

1. What are the "mutant ears" in the chapter title? (*mutant forms of teosinte, corn's ancestor*)
2. What is the main difference between cultivated corn and wild teosinte? (*Corn has large ears and easy-to-eat kernels; wild teosinte looks like grass.*)
3. How did people in Europe use large domesticated animals? (*for transportation, for pulling plows, for turning mill stones, for meat and hides*)
4. Why weren't large animals in the Americas domesticated? (*The ones that were left here after the Ice Age were not suitable for taming as large animals in Europe were.*)

CRITICAL THINKING QUESTIONS

1. What kind of specialized occupations did people in Europe develop? How did they get food? (*artists, toolmakers, shipbuilders; traded their skills for food with people who had surplus food*)

2. Why didn't people in the Americas "discover" Europe? (*Their agricultural methods were time-consuming; people were not free to pursue specialized occupations as they did in Europe.*)

3. Compare the lifestyles of farmers in the Americas and in Europe. (*In the Americas farmers moved from place to place with the seasons; in Europe farmers tended to stay in one place year-round.*)

4. Which lifestyle led to population growth and concentration in villages? (*the settled European lifestyle*)

SOCIAL SCIENCES

Science, Technology, and Society   Have students research the origins of the plow (see sidebar page 150) and prepare a presentation for the class in which they discuss its purpose, popularity, and modern equivalents.

READING AND LANGUAGE ARTS

Reading Nonfiction   Have students make a two column chart with the headings *Americas* and *Europe*, and write details from the chapter to compare and contrast the farming techniques of the two regions.

Using Language   Have students define the homonyms *kernel/colonel, maize/maze, cereal/serial.* They can create a bulletin board display clarifying the meanings of these words.

SUPPORTING LEARNING

English Language Learners   Work with students to recognize and define words in this chapter that have multiple meanings. Some of these words are *wild, weed, diet,* and *squash.*

Struggling Readers   Have students make a chart of information on page 151 showing how the farmers at Guilá Naquitz Cave used selection in their cultivation of squash.

EXTENDING LEARNING

Enrichment   Students can use Internet sources to learn more about the exchange of foods between the Americas and Europe. They can also investigate the connection between beans, corn, and squash: "the three sisters" in Native American traditions.

Extension   Distribute the blackline master for Chapter 24 and have students complete the chart summarizing steps in the development of corn.

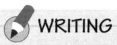

WRITING

Compare/Contrast Have students write a short essay comparing and contrasting farming in Europe and the Americas. Remind students to organize their essays appropriately and offer persuasive evidence for their conclusions.

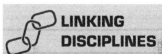

LINKING DISCIPLINES

Art Have a small group of students create a poster showing foods that originated in the Americas and eventually spread around the world. Students can use reference materials to locate images of fruits or vegetables unfamiliar to them.

NAME   DATE

FROM TEOSINTE TO CORN

Directions

Read the information in the paragraph and look at the pictures. Then complete the chart by stating the advantages of modern corn over teosinte.

When the first farmers started cultivating teosinte they made selections that caused changes in the plant. Farmers saved and planted seeds from plants that had qualities that they liked. For example, if, in every crop, they picked out seeds from the biggest ears of teosinte to plant the following year, they would get a crop of plants with big ears. If they selected seeds from plants with mutant ears, they could expect a crop of plants with mutant ears. In time, the traits selected by the first farmers resulted in the corn we know today.

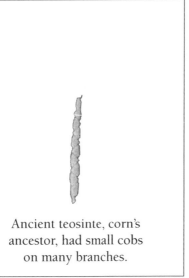

Ancient teosinte, corn's ancestor, had small cobs on many branches.

Modern corn comes in many varieties, all of which have ears that contain many soft kernels.

Ancient Teosinte	Modern Corn	Advantage of Modern Corn
small mutant ears/cobs	big ears/cobs	
ears are scattered over many small branches	ears grow on a few short branches	
few rows of kernels per ear	many rows of kernels per ear	
kernels are hard	kernels are soft	
tiny fruit case, few seedlings	tightly packed seeds sprout many seedlings	

NAME _____ DATE _____

A. MULTIPLE CHOICE

Circle the letter of the best answer for each question.

1. Which of the following is **not** a food native to the Americas?
  a. chilies   **c.** tomatoes
  b. cacao (chocolate)   **d.** wheat

2. People in Europe didn't like chocolate at first because
  a. it was moldy after a sea voyage.   **c.** they didn't know how to cook it.
  b. they thought it was fattening.   **d.** it was unsweetened.

3. What kind of information can scientists discover in paleofeces?
  a. what people ate   **c.** what people looked like
  b. how people died   **d.** how many children people had

4. How much of the world is fed today by plants first grown in the Americas?
  a. over one-third   **c.** over one-fourth
  b. over one-half   **d.** over one-tenth

5. Which pair of animals best represents the shift in the meat diet of people in Hinds Cave as revealed in paleofeces?
  a. mastodon/deer   **c.** deer/snakes
  b. deer/mastodon   **d.** deer/cattle

B. SHORT ANSWER

Write one or two sentences to answer each question.

6. How did European farmers fertilize their land?

_____

_____

7. Why didn't early American farmers domesticate many large animals?

_____

_____

8. What does Guilá Naquitz Cave in Mexico tell us about the lifestyle of early farmers in the Americas?

_____

_____

C. ESSAY

On a separate sheet of paper, write an essay comparing and contrasting farming in the Americas and Europe, and why the differences in farming gave rise to differences in lifestyle.

AN UNAUTHORIZED TRAVEL GUIDE TO NORTH AMERICA: COMPLEX SOCIETIES PAGES 154–160

THEN and NOW

Archaeologists refer to a mysterious population and cultural expansion in areas around Cahokia 900 to 1,000 years ago as a "big bang." It was possibly related to the voluntary or forced spread of religious ideas from Cahokia. Physical evidence from settlements several miles from Cahokia reveal a building boom in which many structures seem to have been built at the same time.

CHAPTER SUMMARY

The chapter invites readers to tour three important North American societies of 1,000 years ago, and compares and contrasts lifestyles in these complex societies.

PERFORMANCE OBJECTIVES

▶ To explain the lifestyles of three North American societies that existed 1,000 years ago
▶ To understand what life was like in each of the three places
▶ To identify and describe interesting features about each site (and nearby areas)

BUILDING BACKGROUND

Ask students what time in the past they would choose to visit, if they could. Point out that this chapter is written to suggest that you could travel back in time to 1,000 years ago in North America. Ask students to predict what they might see and then compare their predictions to the information in the chapter.

WORKING WITH PRIMARY SOURCES

Have students look at the primary source images in the chapter and decide which one they would like to see in person. Have them write a new caption for the image explaining why they would like to see it.

GEOGRAPHY CONNECTION

Place   Have students choose one of the sites in the chapter and describe the connections between the food sources, building materials, occupations, and large structures of the civilization that occupied the site and the site's physical features.

READING COMPREHENSION QUESTIONS

1. What solar events were celebrated at Cahokia? (*summer solstice, equinox*)
2. Where were whales hunted with harpoons? (*Ozette*)
3. In which place was a chief's importance judged by how many tattoos he had? (*Cahokia*)
4. In which place were chiefs selected on the basis of popularity? (*at Knife River and other places on the Great Plains*)

CRITICAL THINKING QUESTIONS

1. Some people think that the Serpent Mound was a ceremonial center. Others see it as a work of art. What do you think? (*Answers will vary.*)
2. How did people at Ozette and Knife River use water and hot rocks? (*At Ozette they put them inside a hollowed-out canoe to soften and stretch the wood as they were building it. At Knife River they were used in a domed sweat lodge.*)
3. On page 161 the authors ask "Will we ever know with absolute certainty what actually happened [in the past]?" Explain your answer to the question. (*Responses will vary.*)

SOCIAL SCIENCES

Science, Technology, and Society   Have students locate a picture of a travois and evaluate it as a form of transport, taking into account the terrain where it was used and the animals used to pull it.

READING AND LANGUAGE ARTS

Reading Nonfiction   Establish that this chapter is written mostly in the second person. Have students point out places in the text where they are addressed directly and ask them to evaluate how well this point of view works in conveying this subject matter.

Using Language   Have students rewrite sections of the "travel brochures" in the first person, as if they had journeyed to these places and were recounting their experiences.

SUPPORTING LEARNING

Struggling Readers   Have teams use main idea map graphic organizer organizers at the back of this guide to highlight the important points about each site covered in the chapter.

EXTENDING LEARNING

Enrichment   Students can use print and Internet resources to learn more about the Cahokia Mounds. One useful website is *http://medicine.wustl.edu/ ~mckinney/cahokia/mystery_01.html*. Ask students to prepare a bulletin board display.

Extension   Have students take turns reading aloud from descriptions of the three societies featured in this chapter. They should use expressive intonation and try to generate audience excitement about the society they are reading about. Students can then work with partners posing and answering questions about details in the text.

WRITING

Narrative Distribute the blackline master for Chapter 25 so students can express their understanding of the sites described in the chapter.

LINKING DISCIPLINES

Art Have students locate and trace the map of the Great Serpent Mound from the Metropolitan Museum of Art's site at *www.metmuseum. org/toah/hd/serp/ hd_serp.htm.*

NAME   **DATE**

POSTCARD FROM 1,000 YEARS AGO IN NORTH AMERICA

Directions

Choose one of the three sites (or nearby attractions) described in Chapter 25. Based on information in the chapter, draw a scene from the site that you chose on the front of a postcard. Then write a message on the back of the postcard describing a highlight of your visit to that site.

Front

Back

NAME   **DATE**

A. MULTIPLE CHOICE

Circle the letter of the best answer for each question.

1. Which of the following sites was **not** on the tour in this chapter?
   a. Knife River   **c.** Hinds Cave
   b. Cahokia   **d.** Ozette

2. The Hidatsa (People of the Willows) made
   a. cup-shaped boats.   **c.** balsa rafts.
   b. log canoes.   **d.** birch bark canoes.

3. Head-Smashed-In refers to which activity?
   a. solstice celebration   **c.** dance step
   b. form of whale hunting   **d.** a form of game hunting

4. You might expect to eat whale meat and have a potlatch in the
   a. Great Plains.   **c.** Northwest.
   b. Mississippi Valley.   **d.** Southwest.

5. Pots made at Cahokia contain clay and all the following materials **except**
   a. crushed limestone.   **c.** crumbled pots.
   b. shredded cornstalks.   **d.** crushed mussel shells.

B. SHORT ANSWER

Write one or two sentences to answer each question.

6. How can you tell that Cahokia had a complex social structure?

_____

_____

7. How did the inhabitants of Knife River transport heavy items?

_____

_____

8. What evidence shows that there were economic classes amongst the people of Ozette?

_____

_____

C. ESSAY

Think of the changes in hominids and their activities that resulted in modern humans. On a separate sheet of paper, write an essay explaining which change you think had the greatest influence on modern humans.

NAME _____ DATE _____

Directions

Answer each of the following questions on a separate sheet of paper unless directed to complete a chart on this page.

1. If the whole history of the Earth was condensed into a single year, all of recorded human history happens during the last ten seconds. The first hominids appear about four hours before that. How do we know what happened in those four hours?

2. Archaeologists and other scientists know what hard work site excavation is. What are some of the hardships on a dig in Africa? What are some of the great discoveries that have been made there?

3. What are some of the similarities and differences between humans and chimpanzees? In a paragraph, explain why the authors call modern chimpanzees our "cousins."

4. Write a paragraph explaining what Çatalhöyük, Turkey, and Koster, Illinois, have in common. Include why both are rich sites for scientific excavation.

5. Caves provided shelter for hominids for millions of years. The people who lived in caves left things behind, so caves are important to scientists. Match each cave with a discovery by writing the number of the discovery in the blank.

_____	**a.** Chauvet, France	**1.** Nandy, a disabled Neandertal, who was probably cared for by able-bodied tribe members
_____	**b.** Guilá Naquitz, Mexico	**2.** "The Kid," a four-year-old hominid with both human and Neandertal features
_____	**c.** Hinds Cave, Texas	**3.** Fossil remains of a young boy who died 800,000 years ago
_____	**d.** Swartkrans, South Africa	**4.** Cave paintings
_____	**e.** Rock shelter, Lapedo Valley, Portugal	**5.** First evidence of use of fire
_____	**f.** Klasies River Mouth Caves, South Africa	**6.** Evidence that people cultivated squash and beans 10,000 years ago
_____	**g.** Shanidar Cave, Iraq	**7.** Paleofeces showing diet change from eating deer to eating small mammals and birds
_____	**h.** Gran Dolina, Spain	**8.** Evidence of humans who were cannibals and controlled fire

6. In Europe, Neandertals and Cro-Magnons coexisted for thousands of years, but eventually Neandertals disappeared. Make a list of the theories explaining their disappearance. Then, write an essay telling about the theories. Use one paragraph for each theory. Include details from the book. Conclude the essay with a paragraph giving your opinion about why Neandertals disappeared.

7. Evidence preserved for long periods of time—up to millions of years—gives us a window into prehistory. Explain how the following evidence was preserved:

   ▶ Ötzi in the Alps
   ▶ biped footprints in Africa
   ▶ cave paintings in France
   ▶ hides and other organic material in Monte Verde, Chile
   ▶ Ice Age animals at La Brea, California

8. Write two paragraphs about either the giant statues on Rapa Nui or the megaliths at Stonehenge. In the first paragraph, describe the objects. In the second paragraph, explain how you think they could have been moved over a considerable distance and set in place.

9. Change and diversity are big ideas in this textbook. One of the changes is in people's ideas about what happened. For example, how and when did people first come to the Americas? Write two paragraphs about Monte Verde. In the first paragraph explain what Monte Verde is, and in the second explain the shock wave its discovery sent through the scientific community. Give your two-paragraph answer a title that sums up the controversy.

10. Put these human achievements in the correct chronological order by writing each letter next to the correct number on the chart. Then choose one accomplishment and explain how, in the words of the textbook authors, "It changed the world."

Accomplishment	Sequence
a. made sewing needles and beads	**1.**
b. painted in caves	**2.**
c. made tools	**3.**
d. planted seeds	**4.**
e. walked on two feet	**5.**
f. hunted large animals	**6.**
g. crossed open sea in a boat	**7.**
h. created mysterious mounds	**8.**
i. befriended wolf	**9.**

GRAPHIC ORGANIZERS

GUIDELINES

Reproducibles of seven different graphic organizers are provided on the following pages. These give your students a variety of ways to sort and order all the information they are receiving in this course. Use the organizers for homework assignments, classroom activities, tests, small group projects, and as ways to help the students take notes as they read.

1. Determine which graphic organizers work best for the content you are teaching. Some are useful for identifying main ideas and details; others work better for making comparisons, and so on.

2. Graphic organizers help students focus on the central points of the lesson while leaving out irrelevant details.

3. Use graphic organizers to give a visual picture of the key ideas you are teaching.

4. Graphic organizers can help students recall important information. Suggest students use them to study for tests.

5. Graphic organizers provide a visual way to show the connections between different content areas.

6. Graphic organizers can enliven traditional lesson plans and encourage greater interactivity within the classroom.

7. Apply graphic organizers to give students a concise, visual way to break down complex ideas.

8. Encourage students to use graphic organizers to identify patterns and clarify their ideas.

9. Graphic organizers stimulate creative thinking in the classroom, in small groups, and for the individual student.

10. Help students determine which graphic organizers work best for their purposes, and encourage them to use graphic organizers collaboratively whenever they can.

11. Help students customize graphic organizers when necessary; e.g., make more or fewer boxes, lines, or blanks, if dictated by the exercise..

OUTLINE

MAIN IDEA: _____

_____

_____

DETAIL: _____

_____

DETAIL: _____

_____

DETAIL: _____

_____

MAIN IDEA: _____

_____

_____

DETAIL: _____

_____

DETAIL: _____

_____

DETAIL: _____

_____

Name _____ Date _____

MAIN IDEA MAP

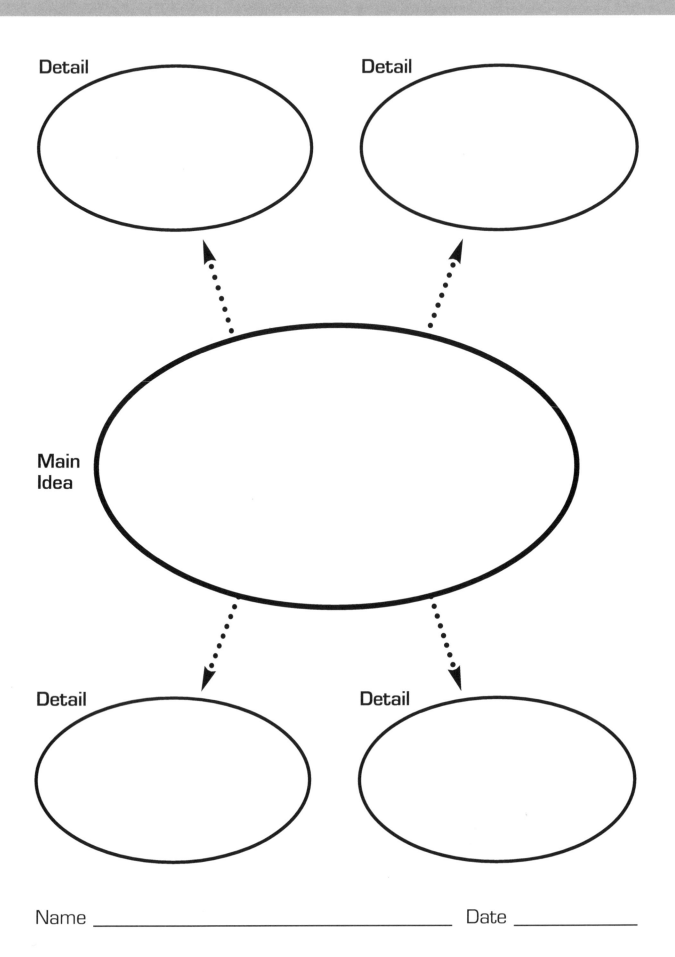

Detail

Detail

Main
Idea

Detail

Detail

Name _____ Date _____

K-W-L CHART

K	W	L
What I Know	What I Want to Know	What I Learned

Name _____

Date _____

VENN DIAGRAM

Write differences in the circles. Write similarities where the circles overlap.

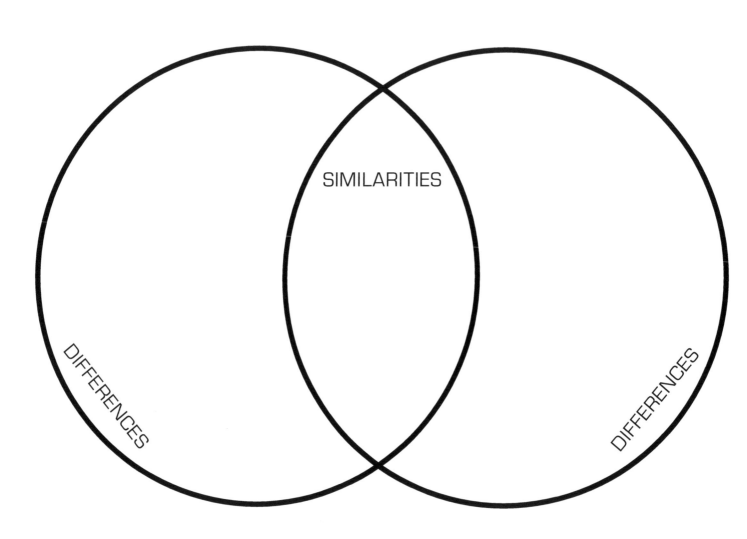

Name _____ Date _____

TIMELINE

DATE

EVENT
Draw lines to connect the event to the correct year on the timeline.

Name _____ Date

SEQUENCE OF EVENTS CHART

Event

Next Event

Next Event

Next Event

Next Event

Name _____ Date _____

T-CHART

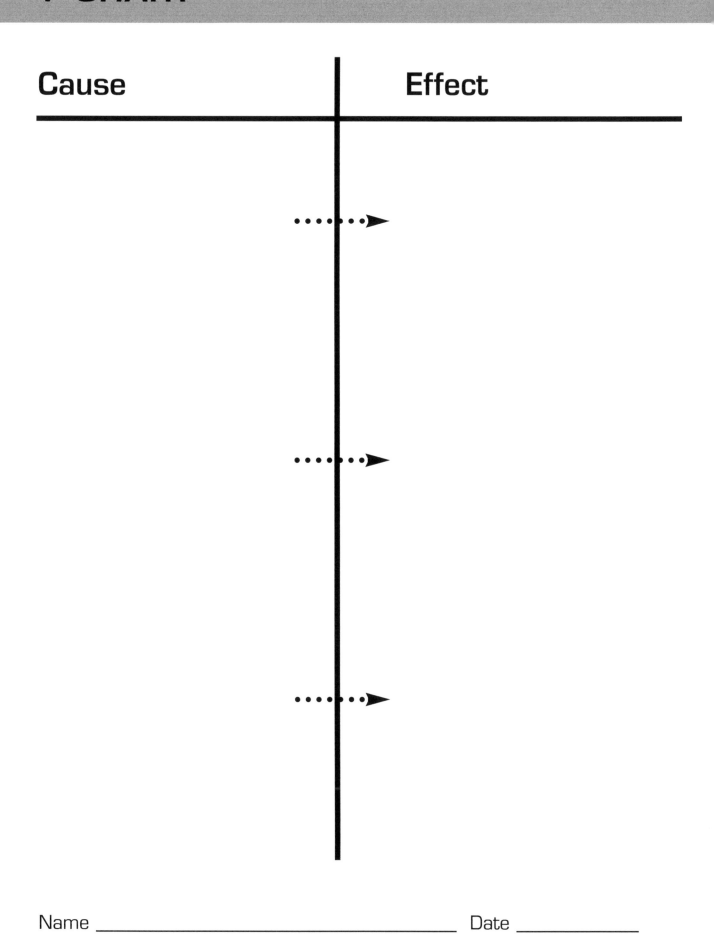

Cause

Effect

Name _____ Date _____

SCORING RUBRIC

The reproducibles on the following pages have been adapted from this rubric for use as handouts and a student self-scoring activity, with added focus on planning, cooperation, revision and presentation. You may wish to tailor the self-scoring activity—for example, asking students to comment on how low scores could be improved, or focusing only on specific rubric points. Use the Library/Media Center Research Log to help students focus and evaluate their research for projects and assignments.

As with any rubric, you should introduce and explain the rubric before students begin their assignments. The more thoroughly your students understand how they will be evaluated, the better prepared they will be to produce projects that fulfill your expectations.

	ORGANIZATION	CONTENT	ORAL/WRITTEN CONVENTIONS	GROUP PARTICIPATION
4	• Clearly addresses all parts of the writing task. • Demonstrates a clear understanding of purpose and audience. • Maintains a consistent point of view, focus, and organizational structure, including the effective use of transitions. • Includes a clearly presented central idea with relevant facts, details, and/or explanations.	• Demonstrates that the topic was well researched. • Uses only information that was essential and relevant to the topic. • Presents the topic thoroughly and accurately. • Reaches reasonable conclusions clearly based on evidence.	• Contains few, if any, errors in grammar, punctuation, capitalization, or spelling. • Uses a variety of sentence types. • Speaks clearly, using effective volume and intonation.	• Demonstrated high levels of participation and effective decision making. • Planned well and used time efficiently. • Demonstrated ability to negotiate opinions fairly and reach compromise when needed. • Utilized effective visual aids.
3	• Addresses all parts of the writing task. • Demonstrates a general understanding of purpose and audience. • Maintains a mostly consistent point of view, focus, and organizational structure, including the effective use of some transitions. • Presents a central idea with mostly relevant facts, details, and/or explanations.	• Demonstrates that the topic was sufficiently researched. • Uses mainly information that was essential and relevant to the topic. • Presents the topic accurately but leaves some aspects unexplored. • Reaches reasonable conclusions loosely related to evidence.	• Contains some errors in grammar, punctuation, capitalization, or spelling. • Uses a variety of sentence types. • Speaks somewhat clearly, using effective volume and intonation.	• Demonstrated good participation and decision making with few distractions. • Planning and used its time acceptably. • Demonstrated ability to negotiate opinions and compromise with little aggression or unfairness.
2	• Addresses only parts of the writing task. • Demonstrates little understanding of purpose and audience. • Maintains an inconsistent point of view, focus, and/or organizational structure, which may include ineffective or awkward transitions that do not unify important ideas. • Suggests a central idea with limited facts, details, and/or explanations.	• Demonstrates that the topic was minimally researched. • Uses a mix of relevant and irrelevant information. • Presents the topic with some factual errors and leaves some aspects unexplored. • Reaches conclusions that do not stem from evidence presented in the project.	• Contains several errors in grammar, punctuation, capitalization, or spelling. These errors may interfere with the reader's understanding of the writing. • Uses little variety in sentence types. • Speaks unclearly or too quickly. May interfere with the audience's understanding of the project.	• Demonstrated uneven participation or was often off-topic. Task distribution was lopsided. • Did not show a clear plan for the project, and did not use time well. • Allowed one or two opinions to dominate the activity, or had trouble reaching a fair consensus.
1	• Addresses only one part of the writing task. • Demonstrates no understanding of purpose and audience. • Lacks a point of view, focus, organizational structure, and transitions that unify important ideas. • Lacks a central idea but may contain marginally related facts, details, and/or explanations.	• Demonstrates that the topic was poorly researched. • Does not discriminate relevant from irrelevant information. • Presents the topic incompletely, with many factual errors. • Did not reach conclusions.	• Contains serious errors in grammar, punctuation, capitalization, or spelling. These errors interfere with the reader's understanding of the writing. • Uses no sentence variety. • Speaks unclearly. The audience must struggle to understand the project.	• Demonstrated poor participation by the majority of the group. Tasks were completed by a small minority. • Failed to show planning or effective use of time. • Was dominated by a single voice, or allowed hostility to derail the project.

NAME _____   **PROJECT** _____

DATE _____

ORGANIZATION & FOCUS	CONTENT	ORAL/WRITTEN CONVENTIONS	GROUP PARTICIPATION

COMMENTS AND SUGGESTIONS

UNDERSTANDING YOUR SCORE

Organization: Your project should be clear, focused on a main idea, and organized. You should use details and facts to support your main idea.

Content: You should use strong research skills. Your project should be thorough and accurate.

Oral/Written Conventions: For writing projects, you should use good composition, grammar, punctuation, and spelling, with a good variety of sentence types. For oral projects, you should engage the class using good public speaking skills.

Group Participation: Your group should cooperate fairly and use its time well to plan, assign and revise the tasks involved in the project.

NAME _____   **GROUP MEMBERS** _____

_____

_____

_____

Use this worksheet to describe your project by finishing the sentences below.
For individual projects and writing assignments, use the "How I did" section.
For group projects, use both "How I did" and "How we did" sections.

The purpose of this project is to :

Scoring Key =   **4** – extremely well
3 – well
2 – could have been better
1 – not well at all

HOW I DID

I understood the purpose and requirements for this project…

I planned and organized my time and work…

This project showed clear organization that emphasized the central idea…

I supported my point with details and description…

I polished and revised this project…

I utilized correct grammar and good writing/speaking style…

Overall, this project met its purpose…

HOW WE DID

We divided up tasks…

We cooperated and listened to each other…

We talked through what we didn't understand…

We used all our time to make this project the best it could be…

Overall, as a group we worked together…

I contributed and cooperated with the team…

LIBRARY / MEDIA CENTER RESEARCH LOG

NAME _____

DUE DATE _____

What I Need to Find

I need to use:
☐ primary
☐ secondary
sources.

Brainstorm: Other Sources and Places to Look

Places I **Know** to Look

WHAT I FOUND

Title/Author/Location (call # or URL)

	How I Found it										Rate each source from 1 (low) to 4 (high) in the categories below	
Book/Periodical	Website	Other	Suggestion	Library Catalog	Browsing	Internet Search	Web link	Primary Source	Secondary Source		helpful	relevant
☐	☐	☐	☐	☐	☐	☐	☐	☐	☐		____	____
☐	☐	☐	☐	☐	☐	☐	☐	☐	☐		____	____
☐	☐	☐	☐	☐	☐	☐	☐	☐	☐		____	____
☐	☐	☐	☐	☐	☐	☐	☐	☐	☐		____	____
☐	☐	☐	☐	☐	☐	☐	☐	☐	☐		____	____
☐	☐	☐	☐	☐	☐	☐	☐	☐	☐		____	____

ANSWER KEY

CHAPTER 1

Blackline Master

Big Bang, 14 billion; *Sun begins to shine,* 5 billion; *Moon splits off from Earth,* 4.5 billion; *Space dust jump-starts life on Earth,* 3.6 billion; *First land forms on Earth,* 3 billion; *All land on Earth in southern part of globe,* 600 million; *Snails exist on Earth,* 300 million; *Pangaea begins to break up,* 225 million; *Horseshoe crab appears,* 150 million; *Dinosaurs exist on Earth,* 100 million; *Asteroid hits Earth; dinosaurs die out,* 65 million; *Monkey-like primates exist in Egyptian rainforest,* 34 million; *Hominids appear,* 6 million.

Chapter Test

A. 1. c 2. c 3. a 4. a 5. c

B. 6. Planets were formed by collisions of smaller objects, with the debris being held together by gravity. 7. The Earth's thin crust is unlike an eggshell because it is not an unbroken coating. It is made up of a dozen or more drifting plates. 8. The supercontinent started to break up and then the continents drifted apart on their own plates.

C. Students' essays will vary but should support the idea that written human history takes in an incredibly short time in relation to the age of the Earth.

CHAPTER 2

Blackline Master

Piece of monkey skull: Root-ape lived in or near a forest. *Antelope horn:* Root-ape lived in a place that had certain grasses. *Toe bone:* Root-ape walked like humans do. *Teeth:* Root-ape ate leaves and fruit.

Chapter Test

A. 1. c 2. b 3. a 4. d 5. a

B. 6. A living thing dies, and is covered by mud. The soft parts rot, and the living material in the hard parts are replaced by minerals. 7. The lower the place they are found, the older the fossils are. 8. Others thought that hominids first arose on grasslands. Haile-Selassie's find showed that hominids were living in lush mountain forests 6 million years ago.

C. Students' essays will vary but should indicate that Haile-Selassie's finds changed our view of the rise of hominids.

CHAPTER 3

Blackline Master

Humans: read, bigger brain than other group, walk on two feet
Chimpanzees: walk on four feet, enjoy eating termites, faces are not flat, hairier than other group *Both:* use sign language, use keys, communicate by speaking, kiss friends goodbye, recognize self in mirror, play games, make simple tools

Chapter Test

A. 1. c 2. d 3. c 4. d 5. a

B. 6. Darwin said that humans and apes split off from a common ape-like ancestor long ago. 7. Chimpanzees' use of tools shows that they can think about a problem and come up with a solution to it using technology. 8. The theory of natural selection says that an animal born with an advantage over others has a better chance of survival. Over generations, those with the advantage would outnumber those without it.

C. Students' essays will vary but should use the example of twigs on a bush to explain similarities and differences between chimpanzees and humans.

CHAPTER 4

Blackline Master

Humans: A, C, E, F, H   Chimpanzees: A, B, D, G, I

Chapter Test

A. 1. d 2. c 3. a 4. d 5. c

B. 6. Apes have to stand with their feet wide apart to balance. Their knees can't lock so their muscles must work to hold them upright. 7. Humans walk; the other animals hop. 8. They stood up to hunt. They stood up to follow other animals. They stood up to look fierce. They stood up to reach a higher branch.

C. Students' stories about the hominids at Laetoli will vary.

CHAPTER 5

Blackline Master

Lucy: height: 3.5 feet tall; brain size: about the size of a softball; teeth: small; diet: vegetarian. *Garhi:* height: less than 5 feel tall; brain size: larger than Lucy's brain; teeth: larger than Lucy's teeth; diet: meat-eating. 1. Discovery of *garhi* was not a surprise because paleoanthropologists were expecting to find different species of hominids who lived at this time to explain the evolutionary changes that produced hominids who ate meat and made tools. 2. *Garhi,* because evidence at the site indicated that this hominid used tools and ate meat, unlike Lucy, who foraged for vegetables.

Chapter Test

A. 1. b 2. b 3. a 4. a 5. b

B. 6. Lucy's skeleton may have been uncovered by rain, and might have been washed away by the next rain if Johanson hadn't noticed it. 7. Johanson could tell Lucy was too primitive to be human but knew she was a hominid. Long study made him name her *Australopithecus.* 8. The antelope bones with cut marks show that *Garhi* made tools and ate meat.

C. Students' essays should concentrate on the idea that *Garhi* had a large brain, made tools, and ate meat, all characteristics that set it apart from the other hominids found up to that point.

CHAPTER 6

Blackline Master

1. Geofact; a battered-looking stone was probably shaped by natural forces. 2. Artifact; a chiseled-looking stone was probably shaped by someone. 3. Artifact; if flakes are found with no large rocks nearby, it may mean that someone had to bring the rocks to that place. 4. Geofact; scattered stones could have been broken by water or frost action. 5. Artifact; sculpted-looking stones were probably formed by somebody with a tool. 6. Geofact; random markings do not indicate tool use. 7. Artifact; only a trained being can produce knife-like slivers. 8. Artifact; the quiet pond would not have battered the rocks.

Chapter Test

A. 1. c 2. b 3. b 4. b 5. b

B. 6. Kanzi tried throwing the rocks against the floor or other rocks. 7. They have found quartz that had been carried several miles by hominids. 8. *Australopithecus boisei* got the nickname Nutcracker Man because of his massive jaws.

C. Students' essays should contrast the random markings and battered look of naturally shaped rocks with the sharp edges and planned flakings of tools created by hominids.

CHAPTER 7

Blackline Master

1. 17; in England 2. 16 million years old; *Proconsul Africanus*
3. 8 years 4. *Australopithecus boisei* 5. Answers will vary.

Chapter Test

A. 1. d 2. c 3. a 4. c 5. d

B. 6. They look at the position of stone tools in relation to animal bones, the terrain, and the hominids. They carefully record the position of their finds to analyze the relationship between them. 7. She wanted them to concentrate on their work so they could find fossils. 8. "Home bases" implied that the sites were homes when there were no structures at all.

C. Students' essays should summarize Kimeu's learning curve and discovery of fossils.

CHAPTER 8

Blackline Master

1. He was thinking that their bad-luck streak was broken. 2. I was disappointed that it was so small and the site looked so unpromising. 3. We made a detailed map of the excavation and recorded the bones' locations in three dimensions. 4. His browridges were fairly well developed but not the size of an adult's. 5. It was an almost complete skeleton. 6. He lay in the water and started to rot. Animals stepped on the skeleton and kicked it about. Something broke his leg.

Chapter Test

A. 1. b 2. b 3. a 4. d 5. a

B. 6. The holes in his vertebrae are smaller than ours, so he probably didn't have as many nerves as we do. One of the missing nerves may have been the one that controls speech. 7. The key factors in finding Turkana Boy were persistence in looking and knowing what to look for. 8. His nose was significant because it showed that Turkana Boy could cool himself even when out in the hot sun. That meant he could stay out hunting longer than other hominids.

C. Students' essays should use details from the chapter to show how scientists drew conclusions about *Homo erectus* from Turkana Boy's skeleton.

CHAPTER 9

Blackline Master

Dmanisi: **1.**75 million years ago; skull of *Homo erectus* teenager and bones of at least five other individuals, as well as tools

Swartkrans Cave: 1-2 million years ago; bones of *Australopithecus robustus*, another branch of hominids found alongside those of *Homo erectus*; also, use of fire

Gran Dolina: 800,000 years ago; remains of *Homo antecessor*; butchered animal bones and flaked tools; cannibalism

Flores: 800,000 years ago; tools on an island;

Zhoukoudian: 500,000 years ago; Peking Man bones; large brains.

Chapter Test

A. 1. b 2. a 3. d 4. a 5. d

B. 6. Scientists thing that *Homo erectus* migrated out of Africa because they had a long-legged walk and an adventurous nature that is typically human. 7. Scientists think that hominids used fire at Swartkrans Cave, but did not control fire. 8. They dated the tools in Flores by dating the pygmy elephant bones they found with the bones and dating the layer of volcanic rock the tools were found in.

C. Students' essays should use chronological order to outline the spread of *Homo erectus* from Africa.

CHAPTER 10

Blackline Master

1. Figures 2 and 3 are butchering a zebra. 2. Figure 6 appears to be making a tool—perhaps to be used in the butchering. It is difficult to make such a tool well. 3. The animal might be a lion. 4. Figures 4 and 5 might be on guard against animals or other hominids. They might jump up and down and point to warn the others. 5. They might need to communicate because they are working together or doing similar jobs. Answers will vary.

Chapter Test

A. 1. c 2. c 3. a 4. a 5. a

B. 6. They found a shoulder blade of a horse that had a mark made by a spear. 7. The condition of the finds at Boxgrove is excellent, as they were undisturbed by water or other natural forces. 8. The length of time they stayed there butchering their prey shows that they weren't afraid.

C. Students' essays should include details from the chapter showing the activities of the Boxgrove hominids.

CHAPTER 11

Blackline Master

1. The oldest evidence is from Krapina, Croatia. The most recent evidence is from Vindija, Croatia. 2. Neandertals lived in Croatia for more than 100,000 years. They lived in Israel for about 40,000 years. 3. St. Cesaire, France, and Vindija, Croatia 4. more than 1,500 miles apart

Chapter Test

A. 1. a 2. c 3. d 4. d 5. a

B. 6. Neandertals had a compact body that held heat in and large nose that kept them from sweating in cold weather. 7. Neandertals' faces were plow-shaped, not straight across. They had no chin. They had bony browridges. 8 Neandertals survived in western Asia until about 35,000 years ago.

C. Students' essays should include details of how scientists think Neandertals buried their dead.

CHAPTER 12

Blackline Master

Behavior: Fully Modern—possible cannibalism, bones of antelopes, cooking food, using and making tools, possible control of fire; *Not Fully Modern:* no evidence of fishing or catching birds, cannibalism may not have been ritual.

Anatomy: Fully Modern—limb bones are delicate like our own, had chins like our own and no browridges; *Not Fully Modern*—bones are fragmentary.

1.–2. Answers will vary.

Chapter Test

A. 1. b 2. d 3. a 4. c 5. a

B. 6. The bones of Klasies people are delicate like those of modern humans, show that they had chins and no browridges. 7. A blade attached to a spear allows the hunter to throw the weapon at an animal. 8. They can burn things to change the environment; they can keep warm; they can cook.

C. Students' essays will vary, but should provide evidence that Klasies people were modern humans.

CHAPTER 13

Blackline Master

B. Live alongside Neandertals; Live alongside Cro-Magnons; Gradually evolve into human beings. C. Massacre Neandertals; Lose battles to Cro-Magnons; Die out. D. Carriers of deadly disease; Have no immunity, so get sick and die; Die out. E. Push Neandertals away from places where they can hunt; Have to scratch out existence in poor areas; Die out.

1. Stringer's research contradicts theory A, as he finds no evidence of Neandertal features in modern human bones. 2. Answers will vary.

Chapter Test

A. 1. b 2. c 3. c 4. d 5. b

B. 6. The Kid's features seemed to be a cross between Cro-Magnon and Neandertal features. 7. Stringer traveled across Europe measuring all the human and hominid fossil skulls he could find. 8. These scientists believe that modern humans gradually developed from different populations all over the Old World.

C. Students' essays will vary but should include evidence that Neandertals are related to modern humans.

CHAPTER 14

Blackline Master

1. New Guinea and some of the Solomon Islands were connected to Australia. Indonesia and Borneo were connected to China. 2. They would have had to travel about 3,000 miles over water. 3. about 750 miles 4. One possible route (from the word *China* on the map, across water to the Philippines, then across water to the ancient Australian coast at New Guinea) is about 3,000 miles, with two stretches of about 350 miles each over water.

Chapter Test

A. 1. b 2. d 3. a 4. a 5. d

B. 6. Rising seas, climate change, and giant beasts are probably the truth 7. The megafauna may have disappeared because of climate change, fires set by the first Australians that killed the animals' food, or hunting by the first Australians. 8. The early people of that region traded from island to island, since obsidian is found only on certain islands.

C. Students' essays should evaluate the details from the Dreamtime stories for particles of truth.

CHAPTER 15

Blackline Master

Barbed spear point: Weapons could kill animals faster and with less effort.

Spear-thrower: Spears could be thrown farther with deadlier impact, making hunting more animals easier.

Beads: People had time to made decorative articles.

Building with mammoth bones: People were making permanent structures.

Ax with handle: Handle made using the tool easier and work faster.

Sewing needle: People could make clothes by sewing skins together.

Net: People could catch more animals at one time.

Chapter Test

A. 1. a 2. c 3. a 4. d 5. a

B. 6. Adding a handle makes it easier to swing the tool, allowing more work with each swing. 7. Cro-Magnons came to this site to gather the mammoth bones to be used for various purposes. 8. Advances in technology probably made their lives easier and less dangerous.

C. Students' essays should discuss creativity in areas such as tool-making, building houses, artistic articles, and making tools.

CHAPTER 16

Blackline Master

Country: France

When discovered: 1994

Discovered by: three friends, Jean-Marie Chauvet, Christian Hillaire, and Eliette Brunel Deschamps

Age of paintings: 24,500–32,000 years old

Subjects of paintings: animals, including dangerous animals like hippopotamus that Paleolithic people did not hunt

Evidence of lighting: scorch marks from torches on the wall

Evidence of people: artist's hand traced on wall, fire marks, skull placed atop boulder. 1. Both are in France; both found by friends who were exploring; both have paintings of animals; both have handprints of humans. 2. Some of the Chauvet cave paintings were 15,000 years old when the Lascaux painters got started. 3. Answers will vary.

Chapter Test

A. 1. d 2. b 3. b 4. c 5. d

B. 6. They found no evidence of cooking or regular human habitation. 7. The artwork was so fresh and vibrant. 8. The artists of Chauvet used color, shading, and angle.

C. Students' essays should be based on the details in the chapter and their own past experience of finding fascinating objects.

CHAPTER 17

Blackline Master

1. The drop in ocean levels during the Ice Age uncovered Beringia. Beringia existed from 60,000 years ago to 10,000 years ago. 2. There was no ice-free corridor allowing passage from Beringia to North America. 3. Both coastal and inland routes are over between 5,000 and 6,000 miles. 4. The coastal route probably took less time, as travel by boat would have been faster than travel on foot.

Chapter Test

A. 1. d 2. a 3. b 4. b 5. b

B. 6. It contradicted the theory that all humans came to the Americas by walking across the Beringian land bridge. 7. The Clovis people hunted the Columbian mammoth with special spear points. 8. Two other very old sites may have been human habitations: Meadowcroft Rock Shelter in Pennsylvania (20,000 years ago) and Kennewick Man in Washington (8,400 years ago).

C. Students' essays should include details from the chapter supporting the main idea.

CHAPTER 18

Blackline Master

1. The excavation at Koster is about 34 feet deep. 2. Answers will vary. 3. The top level is now a farm field. In a thousand years, it might be a city.

Chapter Test

A. 1. a 2. b 3. a 4. c 5. c

B. 6. The mammoths might had died out because of climate change or from hunting by humans. 7. When the mammoths died out, the lions and sabretooth cats had nothing to eat, so they died, too. 8. The first Americans' first pet was the dog (wolf). Graves for the dogs have been found at Koster.

C. Students' essays will vary but should include details and ideas from the chapter.

CHAPTER 19

Blackline Master

Bulges in upper arm bones—villagers pounded grain with mortars and pestles. Pitted eye sockets—villagers lived close together and near their animals. Grooves in teeth—some villagers specialized in weaving baskets and making string. Big neck bones—villagers carried heavy things in baskets on their heads. Wear on big toe bones of women—women spent long hours on their knees grinding grain.

Chapter Test

A. 1. b 2. a 3. c 4. c 5. a

B. 6. It was a place where people who were hunter-gatherers switched to being farmers. 7. Answers will vary but should be taken from the chapter. 8. The first farmers domesticated grain, sheep, goats, pigs, and cattle.

C. Students' essays will vary but should include details from the chapter.

CHAPTER 20

Blackline Master

1.–3. Answers will vary.

Chapter Test

A. 1. b 2. d 3. d 4. a 5. c

B. 6. One possible reason is to establish that the present inhabitants of the house own it, since their ancestors are buried there. 7. They had to climb up to their roof, walk across other roofs, and then climb down into their friends' house. 8. The people wanted their houses to look pretty.

C. Students' essays should include details about the questions about the site listed at the end of the chapter.

CHAPTER 21

Blackline Master

Ötzi: Found in the Ötzal Alps. 40 years old. Also known as the "Iceman" because he was frozen in ice. Clothing, a wooden ax handle, arrows, ember box, and a copper ax were found with him. He ate goat and deer meat, barley, and cereal. He had arthritis, hardening of the arteries, a stroke, black lung disease, parasites, and fleas. He spent his childhood just south of where he was found and his adult life 37 miles north of where he was found. Scientists wonder why this Stone Age man had a copper ax, why he was in the mountains, and why he was killed.

Archer of Amesbury: Found near Stonehenge, England. 40 years old. Also known as the "King of Stonehenge" because he was a wealthy and powerful person who could have directed the building of Stonehenge. Buried with him were one hundred items, including copper knives, gold earrings, stone arrowheads, and a slate wrist guard. We don't know what he ate. His left kneecap had been ripped off, he had an abscess on his jaw and a bone infection. He grew up in the area of the Alps and later traveled to Britain. Scientists wonder why the Archer was buried where he was, whether he was connected with the building of Stonehenge, and why he traveled to Britain.

Chapter Test

A. 1. c 2. b 3. a 4. a 5. a

B. 6. The feathers on his arrows are placed so the arrow will fly straight and spin, which are physics principles. 7. He was buried with many things, which Stone Age burials did not have since Stone Age people did not have many things. 8. Answers will vary.

C. Students' essays should include ideas and details from the chapter.

CHAPTER 22

Blackline Master

1.–4. Ask students to show their work.

Chapter Test

A. 1. c 2. c 3. a 4. c 5. d

B. 6. The remains of sheep stalls have been found, and rock art shows dogs rounding up sheep. 7. The people of the Sahara 7,000 years ago herded domestic cattle, sheep, and goats and hunted, fished, and gathered plants. 8. Farming produced more food for the growing population than hunting and gathering did.

C. Students' essays should demonstrate that the people who lived in the Sahara adapted their ways of getting food to the changing environment.

CHAPTER 23

Blackline Master

1. Polynesia is northeast of Australia. 2. The absolute location of Rapa Nui is about 27° S 109° W.

Chapter Test

A. 1. a 2. c 3. d 4. c 5. a

B. 6. He believed that the plants in Polynesia were similar to the ones in South America. 7. South Americans did not use large rafts, they did not use sails, and the plants were found to have reached Polynesia by natural means thousands of years before people arrived. 8. When the wood used to transport the statues ran out, the people could no longer build canoes to travel off the island or fish. They were isolated. Tree-cutters had no more work, and couldn't trade. Inequalities led to conflict.

C. Students' essays should use details from the chapter to retell Heyerdahl's trips.

CHAPTER 24

Blackline Master

Advantages of modern corn: Big ears and cobs give more kernels for food. Ears growing on a few short branches makes harvesting easier. Many rows of kernels per ear provides more food on fewer branches. Soft kernels means corn can be eaten without being ground. Many seedlings means more can be used for planting the next crop.

Chapter Test

A. 1. d 2. a 3. a 4. c 5. d

B. 6. European farmers fertilized their lands with the droppings of their cattle and other large animals. 7. There were only two species of large animals left to domesticate—the llama and the alpaca—and they couldn't pull a plow or be ridden. 8. The cave shows us that early farmers were still mobile. They stayed in one place long enough to farm their crops, and then moved on again.

C. Students' essays should include ideas and details from the chapter that link farming with lifestyle.

CHAPTER 25

Blackline Master
Students' postcards will vary but should be based on information in the chapter.

Chapter Test
A. 1. c 2. a 3. d 4. c 5. b

B. 6. Cahokia had many different levels of priests.
7. They used travois harnessed to dogs. 8. Whale hunts were restricted to the wealthiest families, indicating a class structure.

C. Students' essays should include information from the book.

WRAP-UP TEST

1. Students should indicate that we know what happened in the four hours before recorded human history started through the efforts of archaeologists, paleontologists, and other scientists who study fossils and ancient peoples. 2. Hardships on a dig in Africa include lack of water, heat, poisonous pests, and bugs. Major discoveries include Lucy and *Garhi* and the footprints of Laetoli in Olduvai Gorge, other hominids in other sites, the hominids of Swartkrans Cave, and the Klasies River people. 3. Chimpanzees are humans' closest living relatives. They can catch our diseases, can give us blood, and can even talk to us. Chimpanzees and humans both recognize themselves in a mirror, laugh when they are happy, use and make tools, play games, and live in family groups. But the differences between us mean we are not the same. We are cousins instead of brothers or sisters. 4. Çatalhöyük, Turkey, and Koster, Illinois, are similar in that they are both sites that were inhabited for a long time by humans, who built newer settlements over the ruins of the older settlements. Not only are both sites rich in human artifacts, but they both show how human life changed over the years. 5. 1. g 2. e 3. h 4. a 5. d 6. b 7. c 8. f
6. Possible theories on the disappearance of Neandertals: Cro-Magnons massacred them. Cro-Magnons pushed them out of prime hunting grounds, making them scratch out a living in poor areas. Cro-Magnons carried a disease for which Neandertals had no immunity, causing their death. Cro-Magnon population grew faster than the Neandertal population, gradually overwhelming the Neandertals. Neandertals and Cro-Magnons intermixed to create modern humans. Cro-Magnons and Neandertals both developed into modern humans. Students' paragraphs will vary. 7. Ötzi was preserved by being frozen. The biped footprints in Africa were preserved by volcanic ash covering them being, turned into mud, and then hardening. Cave paintings in France were preserved because they were in a cave whose location was unknown for thousands of years. Hides and other organic material in Monte Verde, Chile, were preserved because they were covered in a peat bog. Ice Age animals at La Brea, California, were preserved because oil covered them. 8. Students' paragraphs will vary but should include details from Chapters 21 and 23. 9. Students' essays will vary but should include details from Chapter 17. 10. 1. e 2. c 3. g 4. f 5. a 6. i 7. b 8. d 9. h. Students' explanations will vary.

ANSWERS FOR THE STUDENT STUDY GUIDE

CHAPTER 1

What Happened When?
541–251 million years ago: Paleozoic Era
251–65 million years ago: Mesozoic Era
65 million years ago to present: Cenozoic Era

Word Bank 1. It's 8:10 in the evening before the first member of the family of mammals named *Hominidae* appear. 2. Students' sentences will vary.

Comprehension 1. Dust spins into a giant cloud with a fireball in the middle. 2. The fireball explodes into a burst of white light, forming the sun. 3. Worlds crash into one another as they begin to circle the sun. 4. Earth forms, and its surface melts into an ocean of lava. 5. A chunk of Earth breaks away and becomes the moon. 6. The moon's pull slows the spinning of Earth as it circles the sun. 7. A crust forms over Earth, and rains creates oceans. 8. Space dust drops atoms and chemicals on Earth to form life. 9. All land on Earth is formed into one giant continent.

Critical Thinking 1. b 2. a 3. c 4. b 5. b

CHAPTER 2

Interview Students' questions will vary but should be related to archaeology.

Cast of Characters
Yohannes Haile-Selassie, Ethiopian anthropologist who found earliest known hominid
Giday WoldeGabriel, Ethiopian geologist who worked with Haile-Selassie

Word Bank 1. paleoanthropology 2. paleoecology 3. paleontology 4. geology 5. anthropology The suffix *-logy* means "study."

Critical Thinking 1.b,c,d 2.a,c,d 3.a,c,d 4.a,c,d

CHAPTER 3

Cast of Characters
Charles Darwin: 19th-century scientist who first explained the theory of evolution
Jane Goodall: scientist who dedicated most of her life to the study and conservation of chimpanzees

Word Bank quadruped, taxonomy Students' sentences should include *evolution* or *primate*. A hominid walks on two feet, while a quadruped walks on four feet.

Critical Thinking 1.c,d 2.b 3.c 4.c

CHAPTER 4

Cast of Characters

Mary Leakey: English archaeologist who meticulously excavated Olduvai Gorge

What Happened When?

About 3.5 million years ago: three hominids take a walk on two feet, and their footprints are captured in the mud at Laetoli
September 1976: the hominids' footprints are found by Mary Leakey and her team

Word Bank   There are other mammals that walk on two feet—kangaroos, for example.

All Over the Map   Laetoli; Serengeti; Tanzania; Africa

Sequence of Events   1. Animals as well as bipeds walk through the mud and leave prints. 2. A volcanic eruption shoots a cloud of ash into the sky. 3. The ash settles to the ground like fine beach sand. 4. Several volcanic eruptions covered the prints in a thick layer of ash. 5. Rain falls, turning the ash into mud. 6. Sun baked the ash, which hardened the prints. 7. Over millions of years, water and wind wear away the ash, exposing the prints.

Working with Primary Sources   1.b 2.b,d 3.b,d

Write About It   Students' answers will vary.

CHAPTER 5

Cast of Characters

Donald Johanson: American paleoanthropologist who discovered Lucy
Tom Gray: student of Johanson who helped uncover Lucy
Tim White: professor who found and described many important hominid fossils
Lucy: *Australopithecus afarensis* hominid, 3.2 millions year old
The Ethiopian name given to Lucy is Dinquinesh, which means "thou art wonderful."

Word Bank   *Australopithecus*; marrow   Students' sentences should use *primitive* or *fossil*.

All Over the Map   1. Hadar 2. Afar Triangle 3. Ethiopia 4. Africa

Critical Thinking   *Afarensis*: lived 3.1 million years ago, mainly vegetarian, ate insects and reptiles, discovered in 1970s, "Lucy"

Garhi: lived 2 to 3 million years ago, ate marrow, made tools, discovered in 1990s, "surprise"

Both: hominid, found in Ethiopia, biped

Working with Primary Sources   1.b 2. The prefix *bi-* means "two." Students' lists will vary. 3.c 4.b 5.b 6.b   Students' descriptions will vary but should included details from the chapter.

CHAPTER 6

Cast of Characters

Nick Toth: American anthropologist and stone tool-making expert
Sue Savage-Rumbaugh: professor of biology who studies intelligence of primates
Kanzi: stone-knapping chimpanzee

Word Bank   1. Olduvai 2. sagittal crest 3. knapped 4. artifact 5. geofact 6. bonobo   Students' sentences should include *flake*.

Critical Thinking   1.F 2.F 3.O 4.F 5.F 6.O 7.F 8.F 9.O

What Do You Think   This is a fact, because it can be proved by asking Toth, an authority on the subject. This statement indicates that chimpanzees have less ability to control a tool like a knapping rock than early hominids did.

Working with Primary Sources   1. The hominid probably held the tool at the top and cut with the bottom. 2. Kanzi used the flake to cut open juice boxes. 3. Answers will vary. 4. Possible answers: butchering an animal, cutting bones to get marrow, cutting a branch, hitting an attacker, digging a hole.

CHAPTER 7

Cast of Characters

Mary Leakey: archaeologist who excavated Olduvai Gorge
Kamoya Kimeu: Kenyan fossil hunter; finder of many early hominids

Word Bank   Thirty years after this bumpy ride in 1960 through the open plain; The Serengeti is a savannah: it is a large plain with long grasses.

What Happened When?

1960: Kamoya Kimeu began to work for Mary Leakey in Olduvai Gorge.
2 million years ago: hominids gathered at the site that Mary Leakey excavated in Olduvai Gorge.

Critical Thinking   1.b,c 2.a,b 3.a,b,d 4.a,b,d

Working with Primary Sources   Students' sketches will vary but should be similar to the pictures in the chapter. Students' journal entries will vary.

CHAPTER 8

Cast of Characters

Alan Walker: British paleoanthroplogist who has examined many fossils found in East Africa
Richard Leakey: son of Mary and Louis Leakey; has organized many paleoanthropological expeditions
Kamoya Kimeu: Kenyan fossil hunter; finder of many early hominids
Maeve Leakey: wife of Richard Leakey; paleontologist

Word Bank   The spinal column is made up of a tower of spool-shaped bones   Vertebrate means "animal with a backbone."

All Over the Map   1. Africa 2. Kenya 3. Nariokotome 4. Turkana

Critical Thinking   1.b,c 2.a,b 3.d 4.b

Working with Primary Sources   1. line to teeth 2. line to top of skull 3. line to heavy bones above eye sockets 4. line to nasal socket   Students' sketches will vary.

CHAPTER 9

Cast of Characters

Alan Walker: British paleoanthroplogist who has examined many fossils found in East Africa
Ian Tattersall: Anthropologist who has written on human evolution
Alan Thorne: paleoanthropologist who studies the First Australians

Word Bank   1. *Australopithecus robustus* 2. *Homo erectus* 3. antecessor   Students' sentences should include *cannibals* or *ancestor*.

Sequence of Events   1. before 2. before 3. before 4. after 5. after 6. before 7. after 8. before 9. before 10. after

All Over the Map   1. about 6,000 miles, to Flores 2. Flores: about 6,000 miles; Zhoukoudian: about 5,000 miles; Dmanisi: about 2,500 miles; Swartkrans Cave: about 1,200 miles; Nariokotome: about 600 miles 3. Dmanisi: 1.75 million years ago; Swartkrans Cave: 1.5 million years ago; Flores: 800,000 years ago; Zhoukoudian: 500,000 years ago 4. Students' paragraphs will vary but should be based on facts in the chapter.

CHAPTER 10

Cast of Characters

Mark Roberts: director of excavations at Boxgrove, England
Simon Parfitt: archaeologist in charge of examining animal bones at Boxgrove
Homo heidelbergensis: hominids who roamed Africa and Europe 500,000 years ago

Making Inferences 1. The climate of England was warm 500,000 years ago. 2. *Homo heidelbergensis* would have had problems staying warm during the Ice Age.

What Happened When?

1986: rhinoceros tooth found at Boxgrove; dated site to more than 480,000 years old
480,000 years ago: *Homo heidelbergensis* butchered animals at Boxgrove
Scientists discovered three wooden spears shaped like javelins at Schoningen
The Schoningen site was 300,000–400,000 years old.

Critical Thinking 1.F 2.F 3.O 4.O 5.F 6.O 7.F 8.F

Comprehension 1. Hominids would need knapping rocks to make a hand ax. 2. Hominids could have used the bones to make tools. 3. It took much practice to be able to make a hand ax using the primitive tools hominids had. 4. They might have used sharp rock flakes. 5. It is soft and warm.

CHAPTER 11

Cast of Characters

Ralph Solecki: director of excavations at Shanidar Cave
Ofer Bar-Yosef: archaeologist who investigates the origins of modern humans
Shanidar IV: Neandertal buried in Shanidar Cave
Nandy: disabled Neandertal buried by rocks in Shanidar Cave
Lew Binford: archaeologist who has studied lifestyles of ancient hunters and gatherers Solecki believes that the Neandertals were compassionate individuals. Binford believes that the Neandertals had no compassion at all.

What Happened When?

1.8 million years ago: Ice Ages begin
About 130,000 years ago: earliest Neandertals live in Europe
About 125,000–75,000 years ago: warmer period; Neandertals appear in western Asia About 75,000 years ago: colder weather returns
About 50,000 years ago: Neandertals buried at Shanidar Cave, Iraq
About 29,000 years ago: possibly the last Neandertal died in Spain

Critical Thinking 1.b 2.a 3.c 4.b 5.c 6.b

Working with Primary Sources 1.b 2.b 3.c 4.a

CHAPTER 12

Cast of Characters

Hilary Deacon: archaeologist who excavated many sites in southern Africa
Tim White: professor who found and described many important hominid fossils
Homo sapiens sapiens: modern humans; name means "wise, wise people Possible answer: *Homo sapiens sapiens* practiced cannibalism as a ritual.

Comprehension The Klasies River people may have eaten human flesh, eland meat, fish, or shellfish. They also might have eaten wild plants. They used sharp blades to cut open bones and butcher meat. They would have drunk water from the river.

Critical Thinking *Homo sapiens sapiens:* took control of environment
Homo erectus: controlled by environment, ate other hominids
Both: used stone tools, made tool kits, hunted with spears, used fire for warmth, ate plants, used fire for protection, ate animals, walked upright, made blades with points and blunt ends, cooked meat

Working with Primary Sources 1. The pointed end is the sharper part. 2. The blunt end was attached to the spear. 3. The spear handle might have been s branch. 4. A spear can be thrown from a distance. 5. The handle might have been attached to the blade with a vine or part of a dead animal. 6. Students' diagrams will vary. 7. A spear could be used for fishing and defense.

CHAPTER 13

Cast of Characters

Cidália Duarte: archaeologist who excavated skeleton of the Kid
The Kid: skeleton of a four-year-old child buried 25,000 years ago in Portugal
James Shreeve: writer who theorizes a gradual takeover by Cro-Magnons over Neandertals
Chris Stringer: paleoanthropologist whose research points to modern humans evolving in Africa

Word Bank 1.b 2.c 3.c 4.b 5.c

What Happened When?

1998: The Kid is found in Portugal.
About 35,000 years ago: modern humans are springing up all over the Old World
1970: Chris Stringer researches the connection between Neandertals and modern humans

Critical Thinking 1.O 2.G 3.O 4.O 5.G 6.O 7.G 8.O

Working with Primary Sources 1. c 2. a 3. Stringer supports the "out of Africa" theory because he sees no connection between Neandertals and modern humans. 4. b

CHAPTER 14

Word Bank It would help if scientists knew how long ago humans came to Australia and when the large animals in the area left. Students' lists of words with the prefix *mega-* will vary.

Words in Context 1.c 2.c 3.b 1.b 2.b

All Over the Map Compare students' work against map on page 90.

Critical Thinking 1.F 2.L 3.F 4.F 5.L 6.F 7.L 8.L

CHAPTER 15

Cast of Characters

Olga Softer: archaeologist who researched pottery at Dolní Věstonice

Teens at Dolní Věstonice: buried 28,000 years ago

Cro-Magnon: first modern humans in Europe

Word Bank 1. ". . . had come to hunt large, hairy, elephantlike mammals." 2. Early humans used mammoth bones for sewing needles and tools, for building shelters, and for making fire.

All Over the Map 1. Dolní Věstonice 2. Sunghir 3. Anège

Critical Thinking 1.a,b 2.b,c 3.b,c 4.a,b 5.a,c

Working with Primary Sources 1.c 2.c 3.c

CHAPTER 16

Cast of Characters

Jean-Marie Chauvet, Christian Hillaire, Eliette Brunel Deschamps: French cavers who discovered and first explored Chauvet Cave

Paul Bahn: art specialist who notes that Chauvet Cave art was of dangerous animals

Word Bank ". . . the animals drawn in the Old Stone Age caves are hunted animals . . ." Students' lists of words that have the prefix *paleo-* will vary.

What Happened When?

December 18, 1994: Chauvet Cave discovered

About 32,000 years ago: age of oldest art in Chauvet Cave

Do the Math About six half lives had gone by in the torch marks in Chauvet Cave.

Critical Thinking 1.F 2.O 3.F 4.O 5.F 6.O 7.O 8.O 9.O 10.O

Working with Primary Sources 1.a,c 2.b,c 3.a

CHAPTER 17

Cast of Characters

Thomas Dillehay: professor who excavated site at Monte Verde, Chile, and changed ideas of how humans came to the Americas

Clovis people: North American hunter-gatherers who used a special spear point to hunt mammoths

Kennewick Man: 8,000-year-old skeleton of a human found in Washington State

Word Bank 1.b 2.b 3.c 4.b

What Happened When?

60,000–10,000 years ago: Bering Land Bridge exposed, allowing people to cross into North America

20,000 years ago: People may have camped at Meadowcroft Rock Shelter

12,500 years ago: People settled at Monte Verde, Chile

11,200–10,900 years ago: Clovis people hunted mammoth

8,400 years ago: Kennewick Man buried by Columbia River in Washington

Critical Thinking Clovis: b, c, e, f, h

Monte Verde: a, d, g, i

Working with Primary Sources 1. about 64 feet 2. They would have needed axes and other cutting tools. 3. rooms or apartments 4. Students' sketches will vary.

CHAPTER 18

Word Bank "You remember the stories he told of the struggle to survive on the frigid vast, level, treeless region in the north of Siberia and Alaska." The Serengeti is hot, vast, level, and covered with long grass. The tundra is cold, vast, level, and treeless.

Critical Thinking 1.C 2.C 3.C 4.O 5.C 6.O 7.C 8.O

Sequence of Events Climate change theory: Temperatures get warmer. Glaciers melt and oceans rise. Grasslands are replaced by trees. Woolly mammoth can't get enough to eat and die off. Other megafauna die off, too. Overkill theory: Hunters kill off mammoths. Lions and sabretooth cats that preyed on mammoths die, too. Scavengers also die.

Working with Primary Sources 1. Horizon 8 2. Horizon 6 3. Horizon 11 4. Horizon 10

Write About It Students' paragraphs will vary.

CHAPTER 19

Word Bank paleopathologists; tell 1. Students' sentences should include *deduction* or *site*. 2. Students' lists of words with the prefix *paleo-* will vary.

Critical Thinking 1.e 2.a 3.b 4.d 5.c

All Over the Map 1. Student should shade in the Fertile Crescent. 2. There is about 1,000 miles of shoreline in the Fertile Crescent. 3. Tigris River, Euphrates River, Nile River 4. Iran, Armenia, Turkey, Syria, Iraq, Jordan, Lebanon, Israel, Egypt 5. c

CHAPTER 20

Cast of Characters

James Mellaart: archaeologist who discovered Çatalhöyük

Ian Hodder: archaeologist who directs present excavations at Çatalhöyük

Word Bank 1.c 2.b 3.a 4.c

What Happened When?

1958: James Mellaart discovered Çatalhöyük

About 9,000 years ago: Çatalhöyük is one of the largest towns on Earth

Critical Thinking 1.a,b 2.a,c 3.b,c 4.a,c

CHAPTER 21

Cast of Characters

Ötzi: 5,300-year-old corpse preserved in the ice in the Alps

Amesbury Archer: wealthy man buried 4,300 years ago near Stonehenge

Sequence of Events Ötzi died first. Ötzi was found first. Ötzi died about 1,000 years before the Amesbury Archer did. Eleven years passed between the discovery of Ötzi (1991) and the Amesbury Archer (2002).

Word Bank "Before Stonehenge was the prehistoric monument we know toda y. . ."

With a Parent or Partner Students' lists will vary.

What Happened When?

5,300 years ago: Ötzi the Iceman killed in the Alps

About 5,000–3,500 years ago: Stonehenge built and used in England

4,300 years ago: Beginning of Bronze Age in Europe; Amesbury Archer buried near Stonehenge

1991: Ötzi is found in the Alps by two hikers

2002: British archaeologists find the Amesbury Archer

Critical Thinking Amesbury Archer: a, d, f, j, p

Iceman: b, c, e, g, k, l, m, n, o

Both: h, i

All Over the Map 1. Ötzi's location is in the Ötzal Alps; the Archer's location is in Amesbury. 2. Students' legends will vary. 3. The Archer had to cross the Alps, travel across Switzerland and France, and cross water to get to England. 4. He traveled about 650 miles in a northwesterly direction.

CHAPTER 22

Cast of Characters
Graeme Barker: archaeologist who led expedition to Sahara Desert in 2002
Word Bank   1.c 2.b 3.a 4.a 5.b
What Happened When?
About 8,000 years ago: People in Fertile Crescent began to farm
About 6,000 years ago: Shift from foraging to herding spread to the Sahara from the Nile Valley
About 4,500 years ago: Sahara began to shift to the desert it is today
Sequence of Events   1. before 2. before 3. after 4. before 5. before 6. after 7. after. Early humans were foragers, they herded animals, they herded Barbary sheep, they herded cattle.

CHAPTER 23

With a Parent or Partner   Students' interviews will vary.
Cast of Characters
Students' adjectives for Thor Heyerdahl should indicate he was adventuresome, hardy, stubborn, and independent-minded.
Word Bank   1.b 2.no 3.a 4.c
What Happened When?
1947: Thor Heyerdahl sails from Peru to Polynesia on a raft
1722: Easter Island (Rapa Nui) discovered by Europeans
About 1,000 years ago: People of Rapa Nui start building stone monuments
Critical Thinking   1.O 2.F 3.F 4.F 5.F 6.F 7.O 8.F
Make a Case   Students' answers will vary but should indicate that science is about investigation, not about proving a point.

CHAPTER 24

Cast of Characters
Christopher Columbus: Columbus was the first European to bring items from the Americas back to Europe.
Word Bank   1.c 2.b Students' lists of words with the prefix *paleo-* will vary.
Critical Thinking   1.a,c 2.a,b,d 3.b,c,d 4.a,b,d
All Over the Map
Guilá Naquitz Cave: acorns, berries, thorny cactus, domesticated squash
Oaxaca: squash; Mesoamerican: corn, squash

CHAPTER 25

Comprehension   1.b 2.b 3.a 4.c
All Over the Map   Cahokia: near Mississippi, Missouri, Illinois Rivers; climate is warm; land is flat;   Knife River: near the Knife River; land is flat; low-lying forests; warm in summer; cold in winter   Ozette: by the Pacific Ocean; seacoast town; temperate climate   Head-Smashed-In: cliffs
Critical Thinking   Cahokia: many layers of chiefs; family neighborhoods clustered in city; eat mostly corn, squash, and beans; potters and other artisans. Knife River: earth lodges sleep large groups; chanting and praying in sweat lodges; dogs are domesticated animals; fishing is important source of food; plain clothing and little jewelry; different chiefs for different activities— power based on popularity. Ozette: living by the ocean makes boating important; armylike barracks sleep many families; boatbuilding is important craft; fancy clothing and accessories; whaling hunting is important activity; local chiefs give potlatch dinners and pass out gifts.
Write About It   Students' journal entries will vary.